Praise for *Desist, Detrans & Detox: Getting Your Child Out of the Gender Cult*

"With the staggering increase in numbers of gender-confused children, more and more families face a calamity that leaves them feeling isolated, lost, and desperate. Parents turn to therapists for guidance, only to be told they're the problem, for questioning their child's new identity and opposing "treatment" — powerful hormones that interfere with normal development, followed by surgery to remove healthy organs. Maria Keffler has written a landmark book, a step-by-step survival guide for loving parents fighting to save their children from the clutches of the gender industry, return them to reality, and give them the best chance of a healthy and secure future. Bravo, Maria, for your courage and brilliance. Parents everywhere owe you a debt of gratitude."

—*Miriam Grossman,* M.D., board-certified child, adolescent, and adult psychiatrist and author

"*Desist, Detrans & Detox: Getting Your Child Out of the Gender Cult* marks the frightening journey which is faced by many parents today whose children are tangled in the transgender web. This book is a guide to parents, grandparents, and loved ones to support children through this crisis of identity and belonging. Ms. Keffler's book gives much-needed practical and well-thought-out advice to those affected by this very difficult issue, as many parents are unable to obtain support and have often been cut off from their families. *Desist, Detrans & Detox* is the book which no parent should ever have to read, but it delivers easy-to-understand advice and concepts to a phenomenon shrouded in lies, secrecy, and misinformation."

—*Alix Aharon,* cofounder and board member of Partners for Ethical Care; mother; and women and children's rights campaigner to end prostitution, femicide, surrogacy, pornography, and sexual violence against women

"*Desist, Detrans & Detox: Getting Your Child Out of the Gender Cult* is a lighthouse for parents navigating the transgender storm. Keffler's perspective as a parent and educator is unique and invaluable during a time when trustworthy support can be hard to find. The book offers compassionate, practical advice on how to guide and accompany a young person struggling with gender identity toward the goals of restoration and health."

—***Kristen Allen,*** cofounder of Arlington Parent Coalition

"Our children are in a crisis and extreme activists are redefining reality. These activists' ideology is replacing parents' rights to raise their children according to their own value systems. This ideology has invaded our families and the minds of our children, instilling a false narrative that is founded neither on science nor common sense. This narrative confuses our children with its warped definition of sexuality and gender, and with the promise that transitioning sexes will be the answer to their pain and struggle. Science is no longer the gold standard, but the activists' agenda is. Good researchers, doctors, therapists, and educators are marginalized, censored, cancelled, and even punished for speaking the truth as they know it. They must align with the activists' voice, or else. Critical thinking is now criticized. Ms. Keffler, in her book, *Desist, Detrans & Detox: Getting Your Child Out of the Gender Cult,* intelligently and courageously encourages parents not to give up their children to the activists' agenda. This book elucidates the true nature of the cult mentality and the tactics of the activists who seek to indoctrinate our children. Parents are offered specific strategies on how to save their children from this predatory movement and restore them to a healthy life in connection with their loving family. Well done, Ms. Keffler. You are a frontline soldier in this perilous and covert battle for the health, future, and souls of our children."

—***Jeffrey E. Hansen,*** Ph.D., pediatric and adolescent clinical psychologist; director of the Center for Connected Living, LLC; speaker and author.

"Maria Keffler has written a life-saving guide for parents who are faced with the challenge of saving their suffering gender-confused child from what has become a society-wide transgendering cult."

—*Michelle Cretella,* M.D., executive director, American College of Pediatricians

"This book has come at a most important time in our public conversation about transgender medicine and surgery. It is an invaluable help in understanding how it is possible to see a 5,000 percent rise in this putative diagnosis, and not hear the advocates ask a single question about why this is even happening. Family, friends, counselors, pastors, and teachers will benefit from this highly readable examination of what will likely be the greatest medical disaster of the last hundred years."

—*Patrick W. Lappert,* M.D.; plastic surgeon

"If you have teens in your life, you need to read this book now. Gender ideology has flooded our kids' world, distorting their perceptions and manipulating their emotions. And our most vulnerable children are being seduced by the mirage of 'gender transition,' with devastating consequences. Parents, grandparents, teachers, and faith leaders ask, 'What should I do? How can I help the children I care about?' Maria Keffler, an experienced educator and parent advocate, has written an outstanding book that answers these questions. An engaging writer, Maria draws on the latest research, expert advice, and personal insights from parents and 'detransitioned' young people to provide the words and practical steps to safeguard our children. This is a realistic, often wrenching, but ultimately hopeful account that reminds parents—and anyone affected by the gender madness—that they are not alone, and that the truth will set them free."

—*Mary Rice Hasson,* J.D., director, Catholic Women's Forum; Kate O'Beirne Fellow, Catholic Studies Program, Ethics and Public Policy Center

DESIST, DETRANS & DETOX

Maria Keffler

Desist, Detrans & Detox

Getting Your Child Out of the Gender Cult

SOPHIA INSTITUTE PRESS
Manchester, New Hampshire

Sophia Institute Press
Box 5284, Manchester, NH 03108
1-800-888-9344
www.SophiaInstitute.com

Sophia Institute Press is a registered trademark of Sophia Institute.

paperback ISBN 979-8-88911-322-5

ebook ISBN 979-8-88911-323-2

Library of Congress Control Number: 2024942542

First printing

Dedication

This book is for the desisters, detransitioners, and their families. Thank you for speaking out and sharing your pain and suffering in order to help others. Your experiences are real. Your stories are invaluable. You are so very important.

"I started the work weeping; I finished it rejoicing."

— Inscription on a Babylonian cornerstone

Contents

Foreword

I met Maria Keffler at a conference in 2019, where we were both scheduled to speak about the harms of gender ideology. My talk revolved around my experiences as a transgender-identified child, and Maria spoke about what was happening in her school district and around the country with respect to gender ideology curriculum and policies. We'd already crossed paths online a number of times, and were excited about finally getting to talk in real life. We became fast friends that night, and have worked alongside each other ever since, battling the gender industry's insidious attack on children.

In an effort to provide some hope and support to parents whose children have adopted a transgender identity, Maria and I created the video series *Commonsense Care*.[1] I have been continually impressed with Maria's insights as well as her commitment to helping parents and children who have been hurt by transgender ideology.

Gender clinics are popping up like weeds in cities across the country. Teachers are taught in continuing education classes that they must teach gender theory and affirm children's "gender identities." As a former "trans" kid I was able to get the help I needed from therapists and teachers to identify the underlying causes of my gender identity issues. Today, however, teachers and therapists are often actively involved in inculcating gender ideology in children. An increasing number of states are passing legislation that prevents therapists from helping children identify the underlying causes of their gender identity issues.

Children everywhere are bombarded with messages about embracing transgender ideology, and dozens of books encourage parents to respond to their child's newfound identity with celebratory enthusiasm. But for those who see the harms of this dangerous ideology, shockingly few resources are available.

Maria Keffler responded to this need with this invaluable book. *Desist, Detrans & Detox: Getting Your Child Out of the Gender Cult* details how the transgender movement is, in fact, a cult, and provides parents with powerful insights about how to lovingly and honestly extricate a child from the gender industry's clutches.

Maria's background in educational psychology informs this book, but its heart and soul are the result of hours and hours she has spent talking to parents whose children were indoctrinated in gender ideology. She has also painstakingly researched how the gender movement methodically recruits vulnerable children and separates them from their loving families. She has studied how cults systematically target and indoctrinate people, and she identifies a one-to-one correlation between religious cult tactics and gender industry manipulations.

With compassion, Maria has written a handbook for parents who don't have anywhere else to turn for help.

With this book, Maria gives parents of brainwashed children a road map. She offers parents hope and a strategy for getting their kids back. She provides sound logic about the fallacies and flaws inherent in gender ideology, and talking points for parents who may be completely unprepared for addressing the lies that the gender industry has force-fed to children. She outlines long-understood principles of education, psychology, and communication that parents can utilize to save their children.

But more than anything else she shows parents how to give their children a chance: a chance to love themselves, a chance to grow up with healthy and functional bodies, and a chance to realize that no child is born in the wrong body.

Erin Brewer, Ph.D.
Advocates Protecting Children

Acknowledgments

DEEPEST THANKS TO THE many people whose work, wisdom, love, and support made this book possible.

Some people gave permission for their full names to be printed here, others requested that only their initials be listed, and a few asked not to be named at all out of concern that they may be targeted by radical transgender-rights activists. This is not a moot or sensationalized fear; doxing and attacks on people's reputations and livelihoods are common tactics transgender-rights activists use to silence opposition and exact retribution on anyone who doesn't capitulate to their demands and celebrate their ideology. For that reason, only initials are being used to thank the many people who deserve such wider acknowledgment than can be safely offered here.

An enormous debt of gratitude is owed to A. A.; J. A. and N. A.; K. A.; M. B. S.; D. B. and B. B.; E. B.; N. B.; M. B. C.; L. A. C.; M. C., E. C., B. C., and E. C.; C. C. and B. C.; J. C.; K. C. and S. C.; K-G. D.; N. F. and A. F; M. G.; M. R. H.; M. H.; J. K. and E. K.; R. K. and V. K.; K. K.; L. K.; J. K.; V. M. and J. M.; L. M.; C. M.; N. M.; D. P.; A. Q.; L-A. R; J. V. R. and C. R.; B. S. and A. S.; L. S. and S. S.; M. S.; S. S. and E. S.; S. T.; J. T.; N. W.; M. W.; K. W.; and N. Z.

Thank you also to the many individuals and organizations working to put an end to the gender industry's tyranny and destruction of lives and families.

DESIST, DETRANS & DETOX

Introduction

DESIST, DETRANS & DETOX: Getting Your Child Out of the Gender Cult, addresses an insidious phenomenon in today's culture. The gender industry is coercing people — and especially children — down a destructive path of medicalization in the name of "gender-affirming health care." Whereas the percentage of people who struggle with their maleness or femaleness has historically stayed around 0.7 percent (and until very recently nearly all were adult males), we now see more than exponential increases in people self-identifying as something other than their birth sex. The United Kingdom alone has seen a greater than 5,000 percent uptick in the number of girls presenting at the Tavistock gender clinic in less than a decade.[2]

While the strategies and information outlined in this book may be applied to anyone who has been indoctrinated into a cult, this material specifically aims at providing parents the necessary tools to pull their children out of the gender cult. The author generally assumes that the recruit for gender-cult indoctrination is a child or young adult, as that is the primary demographic being targeted by transgender-rights activists and the gender industry. Because this book is addressed to parents, the word *child* is often used not as an indication of a person's maturity or chronological age, but with respect to that person's relationship to his or her parent(s).

Sadly, more and more stories are emerging of adults who have abandoned their spouses and children in favor of adopting a transgender identity and lifestyle. The material in this book may be of use with such adults, but it may not. The author has no experience in this area.

In writing a book such as this one, a constant tension exists between adequately covering all relevant facets of the material and at the same time not getting so deep into the details and technicalities of any particular aspect of the topic that the reader becomes either overwhelmed or bored. Nearly every section of this book could be developed into its own book. Liberal citations in the endnotes offer the reader materials which can be pursued to further investigate a topic that may only be touched upon here.

You may notice that this book separates LGBTQ, which is the media industry's current standard notation, into LGB and TQ. The author and publisher of this book believe this division to be more accurate, as homosexuality and bisexuality (represented by the acronym LGB) have very little in common with the transgender/queer community (represented by TQ). In fact, much of the doctrine and many of the demands of TQ activism are not only at odds with but actually obliterate the basis for many claims of the LGB rights movement.

The explosion of children announcing transgender identities is a new phenomenon, so little data and limited experience exist on which to draw in order to assemble a road map for parents. The guidance provided in this book comes from long-understood principles of psychology, education, and child development; interviews and conversations with families who are dealing with the issue in their homes; common sense; and informal research into what seems to work for families who are not on board with transgender ideology and who have successfully helped their children break free.

Hundreds of shared experiences and family stories went into writing this book. Most of these thoughtful and wise people remain anonymous, in order to protect these families' safety and privacy. Those of you who recognize your stories in these pages know who you are. Concerned parents have been an oasis of support, encouragement, and wisdom.

No guarantees of outcome can be offered in this book, however. Ultimately, every individual has the right of self-determination, no matter how destructive his or her chosen path may be.

No family should ever have to deal with this nightmare.

But know that you're not alone.

CHAPTER 1

Transgender Ideology Is a Cult of Identity

*"Transition is a horror show that will take
more from you than it can ever give."*

— Female detransitioner, who regrets her mastectomy

WHO ARE YOU? AND how did you become *you*?

This may seem a strange question from which to launch a book about rescuing people from gender ideology, but identity is at the root of nearly every aspect of transgender ideology, and the search for identity is the reason so many people fall into transgenderism's cult of self-determination.

In fact, the development of personal identity is the primary task of adolescence, according to one widely held theory of human development.

Psychologist Erik Erikson[3] hypothesized that we all pass through certain age-specific wickets during our lifetimes, which he called *crises*:

✠ Babies learn either to *trust* their caregivers, or to *mistrust* others if those caregivers do not provide the food, safety, and love necessary for the child to thrive.

✠ Small children develop *autonomy* as they learn to take care of their own basic needs, or they fall into *shame and self-doubt* if their moves toward independence are stymied.

✠ During the early elementary years kids begin to take *initiative* by exerting their wills upon the world and the people around them, but they fall into *guilt* if their efforts are discouraged or belittled.

✠ As children move into the upper elementary years they develop a sense of *industry*, either taking on the challenges of homework, household chores, and social connections with successful results, or feeling *inferior* if their attempts fall short.

During adolescence and early adulthood, from around ages twelve to twenty-one, each human being wrestles with attaining a sense of his or her own identity:

> Who am I? What kind of person will I be?
>
> What is my style? What are my preferences and personal traits?
>
> What will I do with the time allotted me in this life?
>
> Why is identity formation so important?

First, a solid sense of who I am helps me establish what I value:

> Am I trustworthy with other people's property, or will I steal if I want something that I can't afford?
>
> Am I honest even when it hurts, or will I lie to get what I want?
>
> Is my word dependable, or will I go back on a promise if keeping it makes my life less comfortable?

A solid sense of who I am also lets me develop meaningful relationships:

> Do I enjoy being with extraverts or introverts?
>
> Do I base friendships on shared interests, or do I prefer to surround myself with people who hold a variety of viewpoints and hobbies?
>
> Do I want people to perceive me as entertaining, or thoughtful, or brilliant?

Finally, a solid sense of who I am leads me to pursue meaningful work:

> Am I more competent with data and technology, or am I an intuitive artist?
>
> Do I prefer analyzing things, like an engineer, or analyzing people, like a therapist?
>
> Does it satisfy me more to exercise my body or to exercise my mind?

When children and young people are in the process of developing their identities, they are especially vulnerable to influences that pressure them toward one direction or another. We know that children have a strong tendency to believe and internalize what trusted adults tell them, whether the message is "You're smart," or "You're a dummy," or "You have a bright future ahead," or "Something is wrong with you."

Much of what we choose to do arises out of the person we believe ourselves to be.

And the gender industry has hijacked this sense of self at one of the most fundamental aspects of being human: our maleness or femaleness.

Gender Is Meaningless; Sex Is Immutable

Until the 1960s, the concept of gender belonged solely to the field of linguistics: nouns in certain languages were assigned a gender (masculine or feminine) that affected the determiners (e.g., *la* or *le* in French) and forms of modifiers (adjectives like *petit* or *petite*) used with them. Then along came John Money, a psychologist and self-described sexologist at Johns Hopkins Hospital in Baltimore, Maryland, who co-opted the word *gender* and applied it to people.

Money is credited with coining the terms *gender role* and *gender identity*. A gender role, according to him, comprises learned behaviors associated with how one presents oneself in public: a man wears a suit and tie, for example, while a woman wears a skirt and high heels. Gender roles, then, are defined entirely by sex-role stereotypes, although Money did not admit this obvious fact, and today's gender industry activists rarely, if ever, do either. Gender identity, as defined by Money, relates to one's internal experience of sexuality.[4]

Money managed the notorious forced transition of Bruce Reimer, one of a pair of twin boys. After Bruce's penis was critically injured in a botched circumcision shortly after his birth, Money recommended that Bruce be raised as Brenda and never told about his birth sex, or about what happened to him as an infant.[5] As Bruce/Brenda grew up, however, he suffered severe dysphoria — a state of extreme discomfort related to his sex — and later described his therapeutic visits with Money as "torturous and abusive." In fact, revelations about Money's interactions with Bruce and his brother Brian reveal sexual abuse. After Bruce's father divulged the truth to him, fourteen-year-old "Brenda" immediately reverted to living as a boy, and took the name David.

Sadly, David Reimer committed suicide in his thirties. His twin brother, Brian, died of a drug overdose in the early 2000s.[6]

A February 29, 2000, article in *The Washington Post* sums up the Reimer/Money saga succinctly: "[Money's] staunch advocacy of gender reassignment in the face of overwhelming evidence of failure and his unusual practices ... remain, at least for now, unexplained." The article also points out that Johns Hopkins Hospital refused to comment on the case, and has consistently distanced itself from Money.[7]

Despite the fact that Money's primary claim to fame is an experiment that culminated in the self-inflicted death of both subjects, and even though the Hopkins Gender Identity Clinic he pioneered closed for thirty-eight years (from 1979 until 2017),[8] Money's theories on gender still took hold in academia. These theories have since contaminated the culture, with further deleterious effects.

But gender has no meaning, no basis in reality, and no objective tests to measure it. What proponents of gender ideology call "gender" is never even defined. "What is gender?" asks therapist Sasha Ayad:

> Is it related to masculinity and femininity? Is it a feeling? Is it just something you say about yourself? Or is it the norms and roles set up in the culture as related to male and female? And what is a gender identity? According to the major clinics and the medical systems which are really pushing the gender theory, they say it's a person's internal sense of self and how they fit into the world from the perspective of gender. But they never define gender because we're told it means something different to every person.[9]

The harmful, regressive stereotypes which people have fought for decades to escape ("boys are good at math"; "girls like to play house"; "boys don't dance ballet"; "girls don't like to play in the mud") now comprise the heart and soul of gender dogma: if you don't fully align with some amorphous idea of what you or someone else thinks it means to be a member of your sex group (male or female), then you're transgender. The entire premise is ludicrous.

Maleness and femaleness are biological facts based on one's chromosomes and role in reproduction. Men make small sex gametes (sperm) and women make large sex gametes (eggs). In humans, the male's sperm fertilizes the female's egg and the female carries the developing child inside her body.

While "masculine" literally means manly, and "feminine" means womanly, the terms are often used to refer to personality constructs. One can be a "masculine woman" who likes to drive monster trucks and compete in cage fights on weekends. One can be a "feminine man" who arranges flowers and sings falsetto in the community choir. Yet the former is still female and the latter is still male.

There is no scientific evidence suggesting that one can "be born in the wrong body," or "have the mind of one sex and the body of another." Neither is there any objective definition or standard of measurement for what being "transgender" actually means.

One's sex is coded into every cell of the body from conception, and is immutable for the duration of life and beyond.[10] When a human skeleton is unearthed by archeologists thirty thousand years postmortem, analysis of the bones and the DNA will tell those archeologists definitively whether that skeleton belonged to a man or to a woman, and it won't matter one whit whether the man liked to hunt animals or rock babies, or whether the woman liked to make tools or weave baskets.

Sex is binary and fixed. Personality is fluid and varied. Gender only has meaning in the field of linguistics.

However, gender has still managed to become a catastrophic cult phenomenon.

The Disturbing Parallels Between Cults and Gender Ideology

Cults are fanatical groups that coalesce around a certain belief or set of beliefs. One dictionary entry for *cult* aptly captures the gender-ideology manifestation: "a quasi-religious organization using devious psychological techniques to gain and control adherents."[11]

Some readers may be disturbed or offended by the reference to transgenderism as a cult. Is the claim that transgender-identified people and their "allies" are stupid or evil? Absolutely not!

To be clear, the leaders of this movement are evil. They know that gender ideology hurts children, destroys families, and ruins lives. They just don't care. But the huge majority of those who fall victim to the transgender cult's lies are tricked into doing so. They're handed phony studies by well-paid activists who claim that transgenderism is both natural and healthy. They're further told that supporting transgenderism is the only decent, compassionate thing to do — that, if they don't allow children to be mutilated through hormone injections and sex-reassignment surgeries, those kids will kill themselves. Such claims have no research data to support them.

Such tactics aren't surprising. As the sociologist Rodney Stark has pointed out, cults actually make a point of targeting intelligent, compassionate people. They do this for two reasons. Firstly, bright and thoughtful people are more likely to ask big questions about life — questions like "What makes people happy?" and "What does it really mean to be a man or a woman?" Secondly, they're more sensitive to the suffering of others, and many cults present themselves as humanitarian organizations.

Sadly, all genuine research studies show that the opposite of the claim above is true: adolescent and teenage suicide is more common today than it has ever been. There are several good long-term studies from Europe, where for decades gender-affirming treatments and sex reassignment surgeries have been more socially tolerated than in the United States. These studies demonstrate that these invasive and irreversible interventions do not in fact lead to a decrease in suicide rates post-transition.

In fact, those studies show that when children or teens attempt to transition to a different sex, there is a 19 percent increase in suicide rates compared to the general population. These studies also found that in 88 percent of cases, children having identity and body-related distress are suffering from other issues, which have high suicide rates. These are issues such as depression, anxiety, autism, and other problems that can be successfully treated.

Yet it's easy for the enemies of truth to spread such lies — especially when they've got deep pockets. It's much harder for the friends of truth to correct the record — especially when "Big Trans" has succeeded in branding critics as bigots.

People can still fight back against gender ideology. But to do that, one must be honest, both with oneself and one's opponents. It's imperative to recognize that the gender-ideology movement is using the same tactics that religious cults use. To counter that influence requires the use of anti-cult tactics, in order to "deprogram" transgender-identified friends and their so-called allies.

1. Identify Potential Recruits

The well-established sequence of tactics which cults use to recruit and indoctrinate people parallels gender-ideology indoctrination with frightening transparency.

Cult leaders and recruiters look for individuals who will be useful to the group, often targeting those who are vulnerable because of their life circumstances.

A teacher and Gender and Sexuality Allies (GSA) club advisor in California was caught on video teaching other adults how to start GSA clubs in their schools. She encouraged them to "poach kids from the counseling department," admitting that they actively target the most emotionally and psychologically vulnerable recruits for LGB and TQ groups.[12] A mother in the Washington, D.C., area attended a "Diversity/Equity/Inclusion" training in which teachers were instructed, "If you see kids who are alone at their lockers or by themselves in the lunchrooms, approach them to talk about their sexuality and gender."[13]

2. **Draw the Recruit In**

Rachel Goldberg describes how she was drawn into the now-infamous NXIVM (alleged) sex cult: "For me, it began with a professional development workshop a former job of mine paid for, aimed at 'optimizing our potential.' This group had no affiliation with NXIVM, but it opened a gateway into a community of self-improvement aficionados. I went for a pretty standard reason: the free wine and cured meats. But the workshop itself delved deep into our egos, sense of empathy, and mental and behavioral patterns."[14]

GSA club members who give sex and gender training in various classes at school[15]; a panoply of wealthy and glamorous social media influencers on platforms like Snapchat, TikTok, Reddit, DeviantArt, Tumblr, and Discord[16]; in-school LGB and TQ celebrations nearly every month of the year[17]; and policies which not only promote transgender ideology but also punish any dissension from it — all work to funnel children into the gender industry's web.[18]

3. **Love-Bomb the Recruit**

Cults shower potential and new members with affection, approval, and adoration, in order to stroke the deep human need for connection and affirmation, as well as to weaken intellectual resistance to the group's doctrine and the group leader's power. Love-bombing creates a false sense of well-being and joy in the recruit.[19]

The GSA club is a community of instant belonging. Detransitioners (those who were transgender-identified, but have gone back to presenting as their birth sex) frequently describe having felt different from the other kids at school, and without a friend group. Joining the GSA club brought instant friends and protectors, as well as sudden popularity. They joined the cadre of edgy, cool kids — a heady experience:

> Tumblr was ecstatic ... congratulations, encouragement, and support was sent my way — something that girl-me never got for being exactly the same as boy-me, save having a different name and pronouns. [My] mannerisms and appearance, which had previously [made me different from others] ... and my "bravery" [were] applauded by all the people I looked up to ... online and friends in real life.[20]

4. **Sell, Sell, Sell**

Cults promise love, joy, happiness, success, and a meaningful life. Whether it's a religious cult offering nirvana on earth or a business cult promising a financial windfall if you stick to their program, the premise is the same: "We have the answers and you'll be lucky to join us."[21]

I recently took a stroll through the halls of my kids' high school, noting how many LGB and TQ advertisements covered the walls. Every hallway had at least one Pride poster, most had transgender flags, and about half the classroom doors sported Pride rainbows, transgender flags, and/or GLSEN Safe Space[22] stickers. No other club or community had so much marketing real estate granted to them. It's crystal clear to anyone who enters that building who the important people at school are: the LGB and TQ kids.

5. **Apply Hard Love**

This step is also called "Establishment of Guilt" and includes carrot/stick motivators to manipulate the new recruit into the cult's desired behaviors. Cult members must follow the cult's strict protocols in order to be acceptable to the group.

Transgender allies must behave certain ways, such as always using the preferred names and pronouns of transgender people, and by never assuming what someone else's pronouns are. Infractions are responded to swiftly and harshly: those who break the rules are called "bigots," "haters," "homophobes," "transphobes," and "TERFs."[23] One who breaks the rules must grovel obsequiously in apology and demonstrate explicit efforts to change the unacceptable behavior.[24]

6. **Require the Renunciation of Loved Ones**

Cults are notorious for establishing in-group and out-group dichotomies. Those inside the cult are supposedly good, noble, and possessed of truth. Outsiders are considered dangerous heretics. Anyone who expresses skepticism of the cult's beliefs is demonized. Cult members are required to renounce and sever ties with anyone who is not part of the cult.[25]

If parents and family members do not capitulate to one's new identity as a transgender person and to the rules required by the cult, then those relationships are labeled "toxic" and must be severed. Transgender-identified people are encouraged to create their own new "glitter family."[26] Anyone who does not affirm the transgender-identified person must be cut from his or her life. The school, the therapist, friends — and likely even the neighbors will help — by hiding the child's sexuality and gender presentation from parents.[27]

7. **Introduce and Coerce Acceptance of Core Beliefs**

Cults use various manipulation techniques to indoctrinate members into their dogma and keep them from examining the narrative: controls are systematically engaged to prevent members from questioning or thinking too deeply about what they're taught by the leadership.[28] Thought-stopping devices such as slogans and loaded language are drilled into members, to be parroted whenever the cult member is challenged or questioned about the cult's doctrine.[29]

"Transwomen are women. Transmen are men."

"Love is love."

"Be who you are."

"Love has no gender."

"Pride."

"Trans rights are human rights."

"Hate has no home here."

"Be your authentic self."

"Some people are born trans. Get over it."

"All you need is love."

"Love wins."

The LGB and TQ glossary of terms[30] (which is probably being taught as curriculum in your local school[31]) is lengthy: ally, androgynous, cis … living openly … pansexual, queer, questioning…

8. **Permit Zero Tolerance of Criticism**[32]

Anyone who questions or criticizes the cult is vilified and labeled an enemy. Those who speak out against the cult may find themselves targets of smear and silencing campaigns. A member who leaves the cult is shunned and defamed.

Raise a question or concern about transgender ideology and you will quickly be called a TERF, transphobe, bigot, and hater. J. K. Rowling received a sustained and powerful backlash for simply stating that "sex is real" and expressing concern that children are being rushed into medicalization.[33]

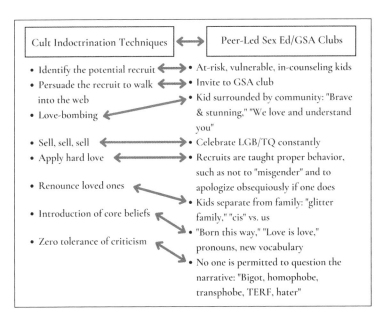

Cult Indoctrination Techniques ⟷	Peer-Led Sex Ed/GSA Clubs
• Identify the potential recruit ⟷	• At-risk, vulnerable, in-counseling kids
• Persuade the recruit to walk ⟷ into the web	• Invite to GSA club
• Love-bombing ⟵	• Kid surrounded by community: "Brave & stunning," "We love and understand you"
• Sell, sell, sell ⟷	• Celebrate LGB/TQ constantly
• Apply hard love ⟷	• Recruits are taught proper behavior, such as not to "misgender" and to apologize obsequiously if one does
• Renounce loved ones	• Kids separate from family: "glitter family," "cis" vs. us
• Introduction of core beliefs	• "Born this way," "Love is love," pronouns, new vocabulary
• Zero tolerance of criticism	• No one is permitted to question the narrative: "Bigot, homophobe, transphobe, TERF, hater"

One high schooler complained to me about his social media feeds. "Everything is about what you're doing to be an activist. There's almost nothing else there. It's not enough to agree that transwomen are women, for example. You have to show that you're doing the right things like putting up signs and marching in protests. Otherwise, you aren't good enough."

DESTRUCTIVE INFLUENCE

One of the primary differences between a religion and a cult relates to the group's effect: Is the organization a constructive or a destructive influence on its adherents?[34] Does the ideology lead to improved psychological health, better behavior, and positive social influence, or does it lead to poorer psychological health, self-harm, and negative impact on society?

⚜ The religion of Judaism teaches Jewish people to give of their time, money, and resources in order to care for those around them; The Family commune cult (New Mexico) demanded members give up their names and personal belongings to the group leaders.[35]

⚜ The Islamic religion requires a *Hajj*, or journey to Mecca, at least once in a lifetime, prior to which the pilgrim must ensure that he or she is mature, and of sound mind and finances[36]; the Gloriavale cult in New Zealand punishes girls who exhibit leadership qualities.[37]

⚜ Christian religious doctrine instructs believers to "do to others as you would have them do to you" (Luke 6:31); the Westboro Baptist Church (Topeka, Kansas) cult directs its adherents to tell homosexual people that God hates them.[38]

Transgender ideology is a profoundly destructive influence, not only on its own followers, but on their families, and on society as a whole:

⁜ Transgender-identified people are encouraged not only to transition socially with respect to their clothing, hairstyle, and mannerisms, but to medicalize themselves via puberty blockers that impede brain development, wrong-sex hormones that ravage the endocrine system, and disfiguring surgeries that often leave patients incontinent, impotent, and infertile.[39]

⁜ Transgender-identified people are taught that if their families don't instantly applaud their new identities, those families are toxic and must be excised from the transgender-identified person's life.

⁜ Transgender-identified people's long-term outcomes are generally not favorable. They overwhelmingly experience homelessness, joblessness, and poverty. They often end up trafficked into the sex trade, and they suffer a panoply of mental health issues, including depression, anxiety, trauma, domestic abuse, suicidal ideation, and completed suicide.[40] While transgender-rights activists assign societal bigotry as the root of all of these ills, such a conclusion is unwarranted. A thirty-year longitudinal study in Sweden, perhaps one of the most LGB- and TQ-friendly nations in the world, found that even after sex-reassignment surgery, mental health outcomes for transgender-identified people remained abysmal.[41]

That gender ideology is a destructive cult must be understood before one can effectively take on the task of helping bring a child or loved one out of it. This is not a phase that kids will pass through, nor is it a trend they're trying on. A systematic and intentional brainwashing has been undertaken upon our children and our society, for the purpose of political and financial gain.[42]

Global Market Insights prepared a study in 2020 calling sex reassignment surgery "a growth market."[43] If transgender people were truly "born this way," then a finite percentage of the population (historically 0.7 percent[44]) would ever be candidates for surgical sex change. For transgender surgery to become a growth market, it must be actively marketed to greater and greater numbers of people.

And so it has been.

Preying Upon the Vulnerable

Studies are revealing that the vast majority of gender-confused children have preexisting diagnoses like autism or ADHD (attention-deficit/hyperactivity disorder), have experienced trauma in their lives, and/or present with co-occurring conditions such as depression, anxiety, self-harm, and suicidal ideation.[45] Yet even mentioning this fact draws the wrath of gender-industry activists and sycophants. In no other area of education, psychology, or medicine does one treatment plan fit every person, but when it comes to transgender identity, one finds that common sense, investigation, and ethical mental and physical healthcare practices are verboten.

Schools have partnered with activists and unscrupulous medical practitioners to exploit vulnerable children, convincing them that hormones and surgeries are their only chance to escape their discomforts, and trapping them on a path of lifelong medicalization. Planned Parenthood, now one of the largest providers of wrong-sex hormones to children, is setting up clinics on high school campuses.[46]

The cult of gender ideology seems to prey specifically upon children, and especially those children in the phase of life surrounding their identity development. The children who seem most susceptible to the cult's manipulation are those who already have strikes against them:

✠ **Autistic kids often feel like they don't fit in with others.** They struggle to understand social situations, and many suffer with sensory issues that can make them feel at odds with their own bodies. The gender industry tells them they feel this way because they're transgender and that they'll feel better about themselves after they transition socially, medically, and surgically. Sex transition is a quick-fix deception that will do nothing to address the real needs associated with autism.[47]

✠ **Kids who have suffered prior trauma (such as physical or sexual abuse, rejection, parental divorce, or a harrowing accident or illness) may have developed coping skills that work in the short term but are ultimately unhealthy,** such as dissociation, codependency, aggressiveness, or self-harm. The gender industry tells them they feel pain because they're transgender, and they'll feel better after they transition socially, medically, and surgically. (They probably won't.) Sex transition is just another maladaptive coping technique that ultimately proves physically and psychologically destructive.[48]

✠ **Kids who struggle socially, or who perceive themselves as unliked, unpopular, or awkward, seek strategies to either overcome or escape their unhappiness.** The child may join an unhealthy or destructive friend group if the option arises, or may go all-in on a lone-wolf or outsider persona. The gender industry tells these kids that they struggle with relationships because they're transgender, and they'll fit in after they transition socially, medically, and surgically. In the near term, this is true, because kids experience the gender industry's manufactured love-bombing as soon as they utter the phrase "I'm transgender." They will be told that being transgender is "brave and stunning." However, just like joining a destructive friend group, signing on to the transgender agenda ultimately leaves a person worse off than when he or she began.

Gender activists and clinicians will use nearly any diagnosis, suspected diagnosis, or vulnerability to claim that people are transgender. It is not sensationalism or overgeneralization to say that the gender industry can and does target any human being who expresses any sort of discomfort, psychological unease, or personal crisis, to push him or her onto the medicalization conveyer belt.[49]

A presentation slide titled "Other Ways Gender Dysphoria May Present," shown at a professional conference on transgender health, listed depression/anxiety, poor academic achievement, isolation, frustration, social avoidance, loneliness, grief, and diagnoses of ADD/ADHD, borderline personality disorder, and autism, among other things, as evidence that one may be transgender.

This is not medicine. This is not therapy. This is not humane care of any kind. This is predatory profiteering off the most vulnerable people in society: children and people who struggle with their mental health.

The gender industry nefariously targets people at the very core of personhood: identity.

The Gender Cult Begins and Ends with Identity

Cults entrap people through a scheme of manipulations and mind-control techniques, and the cult uses its influence to replace the recruit's true identity with the identity the cult wants the recruit to have. This identity-engineering is one of the defining features of cults.[50]

The term *deadname* — the name given to a person by his or her parents at birth and subsequently rejected by a transgender-identified person — perfectly encapsulates the sinister ethos of the transgender cult's goal. The gender industry wants to kill off the recruit's personal self that developed in the context of a protective, biological (or adoptive) family, and remake the recruit with an identity that will not only consent to but enthusiastically pursue tens or hundreds of thousands of dollars' worth of pharmaceuticals and surgical alterations.

The selection of *preferred pronouns*, which indicate how the person wishes to be referred to in the third person (he/she/they/ze/fae, etc.), further subverts the person's true identity and replaces it with the new cult identity.

The gender cult demands that the recruit consider "toxic" and "hateful" anyone who does not applaud and affirm immediate social, chemical, and surgical transition to the opposite sex. GSA clubs, social media influencers and celebrities, and adults who have been conditioned into a misguided savior complex offer recruits allyship and a community based solely on their transgender identity. Former relationships and friend groups are dropped in favor of those which love-bomb the recruit for adopting the cult identity.

Recruits are told they must cut off family members who don't give in to the cult's demands, and enter into *glitter families*, which are typically older transgender-identified people who groom the recruit even further into the cult.[51] By convincing or coercing the cult member to sever the relationship with his or her family of origin, the cult insidiously strips the person of familial identity. The cult member is no longer a son/daughter, brother/sister, mother/father, or aunt/uncle. The cult member loses connection to his or her ancestry. The cult member also loses connection to the past and is further manipulated to recreate history in the cult's favor by generating false memories and insisting that real events were misconstrued or didn't even happen at all.[52]

The gender cult strips its recruits of every vestige of personal identity: name, sex-group identification, friend-group affiliation, and family integration. Recruits become militant in their demands, hostile to anyone who expresses concern about their transformation, and mindless in their pursuit of an alternate sex identity.

These recruits have been successfully brainwashed into the cult. They are resistant to logic, unmoved by pleas to slow down and consider long-term consequences, and combative against any attempt to dissuade them from their fanaticism.

Pulling someone out of the gender cult requires patience, finesse, tenacity, commitment to the long game, and an understanding that you are now dealing with two competing personalities: the member's subjugated pre-cult identity, and the dominant, false identity that has been designed by the cult.

Rescuing cult members isn't easy, it doesn't happen quickly, and there are no guarantees of success. Gender ideology is a pernicious and insidiously destructive religion which has been inculcated into nearly every aspect of modern society, with no good or healthy outcomes for anyone involved. Helping someone get out of the cult may be the most important thing you'll ever do for that person's physical and psychological well-being.

But you must recognize from the outset that you're in for the fight of your life, and your most effective weapons will be communication, logic, and love — not the fake love offered by trans cultists, but real love which speaks truth to power.

CHAPTER 2

Conversations With Your Transgender-Identified Child

"Keep asking questions. Learn why they feel the way they do. Encourage them to ponder hard questions and alternative perspectives rather than remain immersed in gender identity nonsense soup."

— Detransitioned woman whose rapid-onset gender dysphoria plunged her into depression

"Everyone at school loves and supports me! Why don't you?" the teenager yelled at her parents and slammed her bedroom door.

The words *love* and *support* take on very different definitions in the gender industry's world.

Love, in the cult's alternate reality, means giving someone everything he or she wants. A corollary to love is *kindness*, which means never saying anything the other person might not like to hear.

Support is love's synonym. It means full capitulation and participation in whatever ideas or desires another person expresses, no matter what you think about those ideas, or what they might cost you, or what they might end up costing that person in the long run.

If parents won't call their child by a name they didn't choose, nor by pronouns that are neither linguistically nor biologically accurate, those parents are dubbed "unsupportive" and "dangerous" by the gender industry. Such accusations are just one more strategy by which the cult controls its members.

Once you're aware of the gender cult's mind-control tactics — by which your child has been indoctrinated by school staff and curriculum, social media influencers, and similarly indoctrinated peers — you're ready to start having conversations to try to move your child back toward reality.

If you do not ascribe to the ideology that one can have the body of one sex and the mind of another or that one can change one's sex at will, do not let yourself be pressured into affirming your child's transgender identity.

As Goethe famously contended, "If you treat an individual how he is, he will remain how he is. But if you treat him as if he were what he ought to be and could be, he will become what he ought to be and could be." People rise (or fall) to the expectations of those closest to them. Affirming the lie that a child was "born in the wrong body" or is something other than his or her birth sex may pacify that child's anger and bring a temporary and false peace to the situation, but that child will be moved further into the cult rather than away from it, ultimately doing long-term damage to the child and to your family.

If your goal is to bring your child back into accord with reality, realign your child with your family, and encourage your child to abandon the deceptive and malicious tenets of gender theory, your first steps should orient yourself and your child in that direction:

✠ **Assure your child that you love him or her, no matter what.**

✠ **Tell your child you need time to think and process this (if you do, which you probably do).**

✣ **Ask your child to explain his or her feelings and reasoning.**

If you've been dealing with this issue in your family for a while, and this is not the direction you initially took, it may be time to change course. If possible, sit down with your child for a conversation, let him or her know that you've been giving this issue a lot of thought, and that you've decided that you need to respond differently than you have done until now.

Be prepared for anger and pushback, whether you've just begun on this path or you've been struggling through it for a long time. Remember that you're communicating with the brainwashed member of a cult.

As you begin to embark on conversations with your child about gender ideology, it is imperative that you consistently do two things:

✣ **Validate the child's feelings.**

"I can see that you're in pain."

"Yes, adolescence/puberty/this situation can be very difficult."

"I can see why you might feel that way. That makes sense to me."

"I'm sorry that this is distressing you, but I want to help."

✣ **But do not validate the child's faulty reasoning.**

FEELINGS VS. REASONING

Feelings are simply emotions: anger, pleasure, satisfaction, jealousy, embarrassment, confusion, hope, disappointment, and so on. We experience feelings as a result of events in our lives. Something happens to or around us, and we have an instinctive reaction to it. Feelings are never wrong. They just *are*.

Always validate (agree with the existence and authenticity of) a child's *feelings*, because feelings are legitimate and unavoidable, and they generally serve as red flags to point out a situation that needs to be addressed.

> Child: "My friends made fun of me at school and now I feel sad and hurt."
>
> Parent: "Of course you feel sad and hurt. No one likes being made fun of. I'd be sad and hurt, too."

Never tell a child his or her feelings are wrong, as doing so communicates that the child is not competent to recognize when something is amiss with a relationship.

If the child who was mocked by friends is told by a trusted adult, "You shouldn't get upset about that," "Don't be such a baby," or "Don't be so sensitive" (such responses are called *invalidation*[53]), the child learns that being mocked by others isn't actually a problem. That child may never learn to recognize when others have crossed his or her appropriate boundaries, and may be more likely to tolerate abuse from others.

A child's *reasoning*, however, should not be validated when it is faulty.

Reasoning is the process of applying logic to a situation or question in order to arrive at a conclusion of fact or informed opinion.

One parent made the following analogy, to address the difference between feelings and reasoning, when her daughter claimed that her feelings of social awkwardness and body discomfort meant that she was transgender:

"I think this is like a girl in Wisconsin telling her friends, 'I feel awful. I have a headache, body aches, a fever, and I'm exhausted' and her friends say, 'Dude, that's malaria. You've totally got malaria.'"

The daughter laughed and said, "No. She's just got the flu."

The parent said, "Right. A girl in Wisconsin with those symptoms probably has the flu, not malaria. Just like I believe that you are absolutely feeling everything you say you are about being socially awkward and not liking your body. And that's really painful. Other people are telling you that means you're transgender, but I think it really means you have adolescence with a touch of autism."

Again, always validate your child's feelings:

✠ "It sounds like you're uncomfortable with the changes in your body. That makes sense."

✠ "I can see why you'd feel angry about how boys are treated differently from girls."

✠ "It must be painful to feel like you don't fit in with the other kids."

But never validate anyone's faulty reasoning.

Addressing the Faulty Logic of Transgender Ideology

There are numerous and enormous logical flaws in the transgender narrative. As you educate yourself on the topic, you should be able to ask questions that challenge what your child has been taught, thereby leading him or her toward conclusions that are more accurate.

Asking questions is one of the most effective debate strategies for unearthing logical flaws, if the person to whom you're speaking may be hostile to your point of view. Questions come across less like challenges, accusations, or demands, especially if you can keep your tone relaxed and appear as though you're curious and really trying to understand the other person and the issue.

Certain questions tend to draw out transgender ideology's logic problems fairly quickly:

✠ Is gender fixed, or is it fluid? If it's fixed, when is it fixed? If it's fluid, can it go either way, from transgender to "cisgender" and back again?

✠ If gender is fixed, why would we ever give someone cross-sex hormones or surgery before (or after) the age at which gender is definitely fixed?

✠ If gender is fluid, why would we ever give someone cross-sex hormones or surgery at all, because what if he or she changes gender identity again?

✠ If gender is fluid, why do transgender rights activists say that people who detransition were never actually transgender?

✠ If gender is on a continuum, doesn't that mean that everybody is transgender? What does it mean to be not-transgender, if we're talking about a continuum?

✠ What is the definition of woman/man? What allows someone to belong to one category but not the other?

✠ If all transwomen are women, are all women also transwomen?

✠ How do we know for sure that someone is transgender? What is the standard by which we know that it's fair and appropriate for a person to use the girls' restroom, or compete on a girls' sports team?

✠ Why is the right of a transgender-identified girl (who was born a boy) to use the girls' locker room more important than the right of a girl (who was born a girl) to not have a male-bodied person see her undressed?

✠ If people can self-select what gender they are, can people also self-select what race they are? What about age? Height?[54]

✠ Should an employee at an amusement park believe a 4'3" five-year-old who says he's actually 5'7" and 16 years old? Should that child be allowed to ride a roller coaster that's made for people who are at least 5'4"? Why or why not?

✠ Is it okay for a college-aged man to identify as a high school boy and play on the high school soccer team? Why or why not?

✠ Why do you have to wait till you're twenty-one to drink alcohol legally, but in some states a girl can have her breasts removed when she's thirteen? Can I identify as a doctor and perform surgery on you if you have, say, appendicitis?

Don't throw all the above questions at your child in one conversation, but keep a few of them in your back pocket to pull out when appropriate. For example, if your child uses the term *cisgender* during dinner one evening, you might ask the question about gender being on a continuum, and request that the child clarify the difference between *cisgender* and *transgender*: "Can you give me a definition of transgender that doesn't rely on sex-role stereotypes?" That particular question stabs surgically at the heart of this ideology, which is, in fact, based entirely on sex-role stereotypes.

Your child (or whomever you're questioning about gender identity) will probably become frustrated, agitated, and possibly hostile when trapped in the breakdown of the logic. You will likely be called a name (TERF, transphobe, hater, etc.) when the person you're speaking to can no longer sustain a rational argument.

Do your best to remain calm and dispassionate. Exit the conversation when it's no longer productive. You don't have to "win" or get the other person to admit that you're right before you stand down: "It seems like you're feeling frustrated and angry. Why don't we take a break, and we can come back to this later when we're both feeling more calm and ready to talk?"

You've provided food for thought. Your child (or other conversation partner) will probably spend a lot of time thinking about how to defeat your arguments next time.

That's exactly what you want your child to begin to do: *think.*

Boundaries[55]

As soon as possible after your child announces a transgender identity you will need to decide upon and set basic boundaries (or rules) that align with your values and priorities.

Take the time necessary to figure out what's important to you and what you can let go of. You cannot control every aspect of your child's behavior, nor all of his or her choices. And the older a child is, the less control parents have. You'll want to start thinking in terms of behavior management, actions and consequences, influence, and persuasive argument, rather than toward asserting control.

Some people think of boundary-setting as driving a stake into the ground: "This is where I stand. I can go as far from the stake as my arm will stretch, but no further."

Keep in mind that extremes (in this case, either full acceptance or complete rejection of the child's wishes) are rarely associated with good outcomes in parenting. And it's best if all the primary caregiving adults (mom, dad, stepparents, for example) can come into agreement on what the boundaries will be.

These boundaries may or may not include:

✣ "You can dress however you like."

✣ "You can do whatever activities (art, sports, dance, etc.) bring you pleasure, whether they're atypical for your sex or not."

✣ "Your friends may call you the new name you chose, but I will not."

✣ "I will not call you by an alternate pronoun, because I don't believe that's accurate."

✣ "You are responsible for telling our extended family and friends about this, if you choose to. I will not take on that responsibility."

Families with a background in a faith tradition should further keep in mind that their primary responsibility is to honor God, not to honor any person or their wishes above God. One family told their transgender-identified child, who demanded a new name and different pronouns, "You're asking us to do something that we don't believe God agrees with. If we have to choose between offending God and offending you, then I'm afraid we're going to have to choose to offend you."

From infancy through emancipation, your child is constantly pushing outward on boundaries. That's normal and to be expected. The baby doesn't want to be in the crib where you laid him for his nap, so he cries, pushing back on your boundary and trying to get you to pick him up. The four-year-old wants a snack right now instead of waiting an hour for dinner, so she whines and complains and maybe throws a temper tantrum in the middle of the grocery store, pushing back on your boundary and trying to get you to let her have that bag of candy right now. Your teenager doesn't like having a ten o'clock curfew, so he rolls in at half past eleven with a smug expression on his face that asks, "What are you going to do about it, Dad?" He's pushing back on your boundaries.

Good parenting determines where the boundaries are ironclad, where they're not necessary or no longer appropriate, and where they might be flexible or permeable depending on the situation.

We put down ironclad boundaries when they relate to safety, legality, morality, and the child's or family's long-term welfare:

- ✠ Two-year-olds do not cross a busy street by themselves.

- ✠ Thirteen-year-olds do not drive the family car.

- ✠ Use of heroin is unacceptable.

- ✠ Theft will not be tolerated.

- ✠ Completing high school is nonnegotiable.

Boundaries that may need to be removed or relaxed because they are no longer appropriate, necessary, or applicable could include:

- ✠ A four-year-old may no longer need an afternoon nap (even though his mother may desperately want an hour's rest for herself).

- ✠ A responsible nine-year-old might be able to cross a street alone.

- ✠ A sixteen-year-old can drive the family car, if licensed.

- ✠ A teenager should be mature enough to make choices about when and what to eat.

✣ When and whether to go to college might be primarily up to the new graduate.

Boundaries that are negotiable, and which may be enforced in certain situations but not others, could include:

✣ The family doesn't generally let their children do sleepovers, but a trusted aunt and uncle are having a week of "cousin camp," so that rule is suspended temporarily.

✣ No non-schoolwork screen time is allowed on weekdays, but a child is home with the flu and hasn't received homework from the teacher yet, so the parents allow some television.

✣ Snacks between meals are generally verboten, but two members of the family are borderline hypoglycemic and get very "hangry" when they have low blood sugar, so those two can have some nuts or fruit between meals as needed.

When deciding what you will permit and what you will not permit regarding a transgender-identified child's demands, think seriously about those three categories of boundaries: *ironclad* (based on safety, legality, morality, and long-term outcomes), *unnecessary* (inappropriate, not applicable, or only useful for the parents' ease and comfort), and *negotiable* (can be flexible based on the person or situation).

Before communicating your boundary decisions to your child, also recognize that you have control over some things, and no control at all over others.

Control vs. Influence

The younger your child, the more control you have. The older your child, the less control you have.

When our kids were younger, my husband and I could easily disconnect and reconnect the router if either a penalty or a motivator was necessary. Friends who had older kids at the time told us, "Our son is more tech savvy than we are. We unhooked the router, but he just opened his own Wi-Fi hotspot on his phone."

You may decide that the child's chosen "trans name" and alternate pronouns are unacceptable to you, so you tell the child that no one is permitted to use the trans-name or alternate pronouns. But the fact is, you have no power over what people outside your home do, or even on what your kids do outside your home. You will sadly discover (if you haven't already) that most people outside your house (and maybe even some inside it) are blissfully doing whatever they can to undermine and circumvent your authority over your child.

You should have authority over your minor children when they are at public school, but frankly, you likely don't have as much authority as you think you do. In *Irreversible Damage: The Transgender Craze Seducing Our Daughters,* Abigail Shrier quotes a fifth-grade teacher who captures the ethos of government-run schools when it comes to families: "Parental right[s] ended when [their] children were enrolled in public school."[56]

When one couple discovered that their eighth-grade, autistic daughter, who identified as nonbinary, was using the boys' restroom at school, they contacted the principal and let her know that they did not want their special-needs thirteen-year-old in the boys' restroom. The principal responded, "It's our policy that students can use whichever restroom in which they feel more comfortable."

In other words, "We don't care what you think, Mom and Dad. You're not relevant."

That response triggered the parents' decision to pull their daughter out of public school, so they could have control over that very appropriate safety boundary: that their daughter not be alone in a public restroom with males.

With older children, you'll need to think in terms of influence more than in terms of control. Influence can be intrinsic, based on mutual love and respect, or extrinsic, which relies on rewards and punishments. The closer your relationship with your child, the more intrinsic influence you will have. The more severely strained your relationship, the less intrinsic influence you will have.

In the next chapter we'll talk about some ways to improve relationships, and hopefully increase the amount of intrinsic influence you have with your child. When people feel acknowledged, valued, and appreciated, they tend to want to do things that will continue to bring them acknowledgment, value, and appreciation.

Extrinsic influence is what you must use to enforce boundaries (rules) that your child will almost certainly push back on. This is where some motivation theory becomes vital to your work.

Motivation Theory

First things first. Please understand that you have no real control over anyone but yourself. It's almost impossible to force people to do something they don't want to do. You can, however, engineer the circumstances around another person in your sphere of influence in such a way that you encourage him or her to want to do what you want done.

How do you tweak someone's circumstances in order to make your desires more favorable in their eyes? One way is by harnessing motivations.

When my son was thirteen, he discovered that a particular sound from a certain science fiction show gives me the creeps. I have a visceral fear response to it. My son took perverse glee in walking up behind me and making that noise.

Usually, indifference will extinguish an unwelcome behavior. If the instigator gets no reaction from his target, he'll usually get bored and quit trying. But this particular noise provoked such gut-level angst in me, I needed to persuade the kid to stop tormenting me immediately. So I told him, "My son, every time I hear you make that noise, I'm going to kiss you in public."

His eyes got big as two golf balls and the corners of his mouth fell. He said, "Oh, please no. Please don't do that. I'll never make that noise again."

And he never did.

However, my husband also heard the threat I made to our son. Hubs' eyes lit up, and the corners of his mouth stretched toward his ears. "Is that the same for me? Every time I make that noise, you'll kiss me in public?!?"

And right there one discovers the heart of motivation theory: What motivates us is the reason *why* we do what we do. It's the driving force behind doing what's necessary to get what we most want.

People have different motivations: money, fame, sex, power, control, fear, or to be perceived a certain way, to name just a few. One of my teenager's (and most teenagers') primary motivations is to be viewed positively by peers. Because I recognized that underlying motivation, I could craft exactly the right consequences which would threaten attainment of my son's being-cool goal: mother's kisses are social death.

My husband, on the other hand, thinks I'm pretty. He likes the idea of getting kissed by his wife in front of other people. His motivations are radically different from the boy's. Therefore, what came across as a *threat* to our son (public displays of affection) was perceived by Hubs as an *offer*.

Motivation theory is pretty simple. There are behaviors that you either want to encourage (*reinforce*) or discourage (*extinguish*). You have two methods by which to *reinforce* or *extinguish* a behavior: you can provide something to the other person (*give*), or you can withhold something (*remove*). That something may be either *wanted* or *unwanted*. This chart shows what effect the combinations are likely to have on the target behavior:

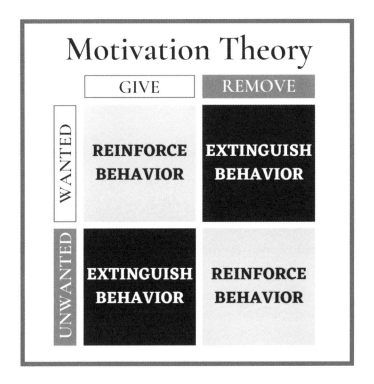

When you link someone's specific behavior to obtaining something that person wants or having something unwanted removed, you encourage the person to continue (i.e., you *reinforce*) that behavior.

Conversely, removing something a person wants or providing something they don't want in connection with a particular behavior tends to have the effect of discouraging (or *extinguishing*) that behavior.

In the example above, the sci-fi noise was the behavior I wanted extinguished. I threatened to *give* my son something he *did not want* (public kisses from Mom) in order to *discourage* him from making that noise again.

On the other hand, my husband *wants* his wife to *give* him smooches, so that consequence would serve to *encourage* the behavior (making the noise) if I applied it to him. (Which I did not.)

If you can figure out what motivates a person, you can get him or her to do just about anything you want. (Please use these powers for good, and not for evil.)

To harness motivation theory:

1. **Pinpoint the behavior you want to extinguish or reinforce.**

   I want my child to stop leaving his dirty clothes on the floor *(behavior to extinguish)* and start putting them in the hamper *(behavior to reinforce)*.

2. **Identify what motivation is currently at work.** (This may inform step 3.)

   Regarding the dirty clothes, it's likely nothing but simple *laziness* coupled with no reason to want to change the behavior.

3. **Brainstorm some possible ways to reinforce or extinguish the behavior by finding a more powerful motivator than is currently at work.**

   a. Remove Something Wanted *(Extinguish)*: Charge the child twenty-five cents for every item of clothing you have to pick up.

   b. Remove Something Unwanted *(Reinforce)*: If all clothes make it into the basket for a week, he gets to skip a household chore he usually has to do.

    c. Give Something Wanted *(Reinforce)*: If all clothes make it into the basket for a week, he gets an extra half hour of media time.

    d. Give Something Unwanted *(Extinguish)*: For every item of clothing Mom or Dad has to pick up the child gets five minutes of massaging Mom's or Dad's feet.

4. **Pick the one that best fits you, your child, and the situation.**

   The child is all about money, so A.

   The child wants nothing more in the world than to lie on the couch, so B.

   Given the chance, the child would live inside the computer, so C.

   Mom's and Dad's feet hurt a lot, so D.

Cult indoctrination is much more serious and pernicious than failing to put clothes in the hamper, but the strategy to manage behaviors still works the same.

Say, for example, you want your transgender-identified child to stop ignoring you when you use her given name rather than calling her by her chosen "trans" name. The target behavior you want to extinguish is *ignoring her given name*. So, if you call her for dinner and she ignores you, instead of going to find her or giving in and calling her to the table by her preferred name, you might let her miss a few dinners. By *removing* something *wanted* (dinner), you may *extinguish* (or discourage) the target behavior, which is your daughter ignoring her given name.

Your child may have a stronger will to fight you on gender behavior because his or her motivations now revolve around maintaining the cult identity and pleasing the gender community. Therefore, it is imperative that you start working to realign your child with the family so that the child desires to be acknowledged, valued, and appreciated by you to a greater degree than he or she desires those things from the cult.

CHAPTER 3

Your Relationship with Your Transgender-Identified Child

"Get close in relationship."

— Parent of an autistic detransitioner

IF YOUR OLDER CHILD has already cut you out of his or her life, you're in a much more difficult position than is a parent of a younger child who still lives at home. But in either case, your first goal must be to (re)establish communication and work toward getting the child to understand that even though you may disagree about some things, you still love and want what is best for him or her.

The gender industry has convinced its recruits that if parents do not fully capitulate to transgender ideology, they do not love their children. This is one of many *false dichotomies*[57] this cult utilizes to exert control over its community. A false dichotomy is a fallacy in which only two options are presented, whereas many others actually exist:

✠ If we don't let transgender-identified kids use the restroom of their choice, they can't go to the restroom at all. (Untrue. No child has ever been prevented from using the restroom at school, but everyone has been required to use the restroom that matches his or her physiology.)

✠ People who say that children shouldn't be given cross-sex hormones think that transgender people shouldn't exist. (These two have nothing to do with each other. And what does it mean to think someone "shouldn't exist"? Does it mean one thinks that the category doesn't exist? Or that people in that category should be killed? Definitions are often disregarded when it comes to gender ideology.)

✠ Parents who don't want their kids to be transgender throw their kids out of the house if they "come out." (Although this happens, it is not the norm. In fact, it may be more common for transgender-identified children to reject their families than it is for them to be rejected by their families.[58])

A great many schools, therapists, healthcare professionals, and people in society at large have swallowed these lies, and they will work against you out of a misguided sense of heroism.

The gender industry tells people in positions of influence that they might be the only "safe space" in a transgender-identified child's life, thereby encouraging these self-appointed saviors to deceive and undermine parents toward getting the child onto the path of medicalization. These brainwashed saboteurs genuinely think they're being noble.

Your child has fallen into this cult because of some kind of vulnerability; there is something the child needs or wants that he or she lacks, and gender ideology swooped in to fill that void. You need to figure out what appeals to the child about the idea of changing sexes, and why. (We will investigate this in chapter 4.)

But before you try to talk your child out of faith in transgender ideology, make a deliberate effort to improve your communication skills, even if you think you already have a good rapport with your child. To get your child to talk, you have to convince him or her that you're really listening.[59]

This is harder than it sounds.

Eleven Crucial Relationship Skills

Few of us are as adept and sensitive at managing our relationships as we think we are, or as we might like to be. We maintain our connections to others — family members, friends, colleagues — through interacting with them, and much of human interaction (arguably all of it) comes down to how we communicate.

Communication isn't simply the exchange of information; meaningful interaction is how we know others and become known to them. We very often miss the most important messages others try to convey to us because we simply don't know how to listen well.

Developing acute and perceptive listening skills is imperative for you to get your child back. Your child must feel heard and known by you before he or she will ever transfer allegiance from the gender cult back to you.

1. **Ask questions.**

   Resist the urge to make statements or demands, or to provide information (unless specifically asked for it), especially at the outset of this journey. Your child believes that he or she is more informed than you are about gender ideology, and that's probably accurate. By the time you discover that your child has adopted a transgender identity, you are likely far behind the curve with respect to the number of hours spent investigating this ideology. Most everything the child has learned is deceptive and malignant, but it's still information that you don't have.

"Can you tell me more about being transgender/nonbinary/genderfluid? I want to understand."

"When did you begin to believe that you might be transgender? Did some event or experience precipitate that?"

"What makes you so certain that this is who you are? This really seems out of left field to me, so I need some help making the connections that you've made."

2. **Do not criticize.**

Much of what your child says will sound absolutely ridiculous. You may want to laugh, snort, roll your eyes, shake your head, or say, "This is the stupidest thing I've ever heard in my life."

Don't do any of that.

If you have to sit on your hands, close your eyes, bite the inside of your cheek, or count to fifty (or 250) before you can respond respectfully, do it.

If you're reading this book, your end goal is probably for your child to recant faith in this ideology and accept his or her birth sex as reality. For that to happen, your child must know that you are trustworthy, and a soft place to land. If you have mocked, bullied, or belittled your child — around this issue, or in any other way — you will make it much more difficult for that child to ever admit to having been wrong about anything.

Your child needs to anticipate that you will be respectful and loving, no matter what.

Instead of criticizing, say:

"This doesn't make sense to me, but I'm trying to understand."

"I'm having a really hard time with this, but I can see that it's very important to you."

"I'm going to need some time to think and process this. Thank you for being patient with me."

3. **Use I-statements when talking about your feelings.**
You-statements are accusatory and put the other person on the defensive:

"You are making things so difficult."

"You don't know what you're talking about."

"Can't you see how much you're hurting everyone?"

I-statements take responsibility for yourself, your feelings, and your part of the situation:

"I'm having a hard time with this."

"I don't understand how you've come to this conclusion."

"I feel really sad and scared about this situation."

Keep in mind that feelings themselves are never wrong, although feelings can lead to wrong conclusions. By starting sentences about your feelings with "I" rather than "you," the conversation is less likely to devolve into anger and finger-pointing.

4. **Receive feedback with humility.**

Your child is likely to say some things to and about you that hurt or inspire anger. Some of what your child says may be true, while some may be untrue. It might take some time and reflection to decide which is which, and that's okay. In the moment that the child is giving you feedback, however, receive it graciously and with as little emotion as possible:

"Thank you for telling me that. I'll think about it."

"I don't remember that happening, but if it did I'm really sorry."

"I appreciate you having the courage to say that. I'm not sure I agree, but I will consider it."

5. **Be present and participate in the conversation.**

Unfortunately, you can't force a meaningful conversation to happen on your timetable. You can invite it, you can offer it, you can attempt it, but it won't happen until your child is ready for it to happen.

Therefore, you must make spaces for conversations to start, and be intentional about watching for opportunities to emerge.

Whenever your child speaks to you — about anything — stop whatever you are doing, look directly at your child, and make it obvious that you are engaged in the conversation. Put your phone down — preferably in your pocket or on the desk so it's not even in your hand — and listen to your child.

Ask questions. Nod when your child speaks. Rephrase what you heard and ask if you understood correctly. Don't end the conversation because you're busy or distracted or uninterested. Keep the conversation going, if you can, until the child chooses to exit. Only step away or stop the conversation if you absolutely must because of a scheduling commitment, or if you feel like you aren't able to continue while being calm and respectful.

6. **Step away for a break if you need to.**

When you start having earnest discussions about gender ideology, you're going to struggle. This cult's beliefs are bizarre to anyone with a clear understanding of biology and reality. It can be infuriating to discover that your child has been indoctrinated by institutions and people that you trusted. The very real implications of where a transgender-identified child is headed are terrifying.

You're swimming in an emotional soup of confusion, anger, and terror. You can say that to your child, but do so as calmly as possible:

"I'm feeling upset right now, and I need to take a break so I can calm down and think more clearly. I want to come back and talk more, but I need to stop for right now."

"Can we push the pause button on this? This is really important, and I want to make sure I'm in a frame of mind that will help make this a positive and productive conversation. I'm not in that frame of mind right now."

7. **Don't interrupt.**

Holding your tongue while your child is talking will be a challenge, because you will hear things that make no sense, and you will hear things that simply aren't accurate.

One exasperating and frustrating aspect of cult identification is the fact that cult members nearly always reinvent history.[60] Your child will almost certainly say that he or she has felt this way since infancy, although you never saw a whisper of it. Your child will talk about all the ways people at school and online are loving and supportive and full of admiration, and juxtapose all those rainbows and sunbeams against how miserable and hateful life at home is. Your child may talk about abuse you perpetrated, which you know didn't happen. (If it did happen, skip down to number 10 below.)

The typical coming-out script usually contains some or all of these claims:

"I've felt this way for a long time (or my whole life) but was afraid to tell you."

"I don't enjoy doing (X, Y, Z) that other girls/boys like, so I'm transgender." (Even if the child liked these things previously/recently.)

"I hate myself (my body) and I'm depressed."

"I'll run away if you don't support my transition."

"I'll commit suicide if I don't transition."

"I'm angry at you for hiding from me the fact that transgender people exist."

Any of the above may be true or untrue. The child may say these things because he or she has been provided this very common script by trans activists or other trans victims at school or online. The child may or may not believe that the statements are true.

If a child expresses suicidal or self-harm ideation, do take that seriously. But be aware that threats of suicide can be a manipulation device that the gender cult teaches its recruits to utilize in order to get what they want from their parents.[61]

Do your best to be silent while the child is talking. Wait until it's your turn to raise your questions and make your points. If your child tries to cut you off while you're talking, you can calmly say, "I listened without interrupting while you were sharing your thoughts. Please extend me that same courtesy."

8. **Check your tone.**

Much of what we communicate to others comes across as nonverbally.[62]

Try to listen to yourself when you talk, especially if you're angry or upset. What tone do you take? Do you raise your voice and exhibit more threatening body language? Do you stand up to get above the other person? Do you lean forward or reach toward the other person with strong gestures, or develop a red face as your heartbeat accelerates?

None of these things are conducive to a productive conversation. They are fight responses. If you see yourself in the above descriptions (or if others tell you this is how they see you) you may need to take control of yourself and reform your behaviors:

> Relax your facial and arm muscles.

> Take deep breaths to slow your heart rate.

> Count to ten before you speak.

> Intentionally lower your vocal pitch and volume.

> Close your eyes momentarily and imagine yourself looking calm and in control.

> Take a break, if you need to, in order to regain control of yourself.

Some people lean the opposite way when they're angry or anxious: they shut down, go cold, and/or turn passive-aggressive.[63] If you recognize this behavior in yourself, or others tell you that this is how you behave, it's equally important that you learn better communication strategies. The same self-control practices described above are a good place to start.

9. **Be appreciative.**

It's hard to be angry or combative with someone who appreciates you. Find things to admire and praise about your child, not just when you're engaged in a serious conversation, but all the time, everywhere. If your child empties the dishwasher, say, "Thank you. I so appreciate your help around the house." Make sure you are sincere with your praise, and try to focus more on what the child does than on who he or she is. Praising something people have power over — such as their hard work, tenacity, or ethical standards — strengthens those positive attributes, while complimenting people on attributes they can't control — like their intelligence, beauty, or other people's opinion of them — tends to make them less willing to take risks in that area, and more fearful of losing admiration for those things.[64]

If your child has a special talent or skill, like art, ask for a favor in that arena. Research has shown that, contrary to what we might expect, people feel more warmly toward someone *for whom* they have done a favor. It's called the *Benjamin Franklin effect*.[65] "Hey, do you have time to do a graphic for this presentation I have at work next week? You do such fantastic designs; it would be a big help to me."

10. **Apologize if you need to.**

No parent is perfect and no family is flawless. You've done things wrong in your parenting journey; every parent has.

Apologize for those wrongs. (And get further help for yourself if there's a destructive pattern of such behavior in your relationships.)

Some people mistakenly believe that apologizing weakens their stature or reputation with others, but nothing could be further from the truth. When we admit our flaws and ask forgiveness for our missteps, we strengthen the relationship. We also model responsibility and maturity, showing our kids that saying "I'm sorry" is the right thing to do when we mess up. (Would that more of our celebrities and statesmen had learned this at home.)

There's also strong evidence from neuroscience that new neural pathways are formed during periods of relational healing, and that relationships themselves grow stronger when we've done the mental and emotional work necessary to forgive and be forgiven.[66]

11. Express love.

Say, "I love you." Say it often, say it sincerely, and say it whether or not it's reciprocated. Perhaps the biggest lie these kids are told is that their parents don't love them.

One parent tells this story, about when she addressed the real meaning of *love* with her transgender-identified daughter, whom she had pulled from public school (under extreme duress) to homeschool.

"Emma" refused to enter the classroom for her once-weekly homeschool co-op, choosing instead to sit alone outside for the entire school day. Toward the end of the afternoon, her mother went outside to talk to her.

"What do you want, Emma?" I asked her.

"I want to go back to school where people care about me!" she yelled.

Fury rose up from the center of my being.

Where people 'care about' her?

I wanted to scream, considering all she'd already put our family through.

Here I was, spending the day crying, sitting outside a building we both should have been inside, after giving up every self-fulfilling part of my own life so I could try to save her from herself and from the liars who did this to her.

Yet those liars supposedly loved her more than I did.

"Do you really think those people care about you, Emma?"

I knew what I was about to say might wound her deeply. But she needed to hear it.

"Have you heard from any of those people who care so much about you? Because I haven't. Not one teacher has called me to ask about you. Not one of the staff or the counselors have checked in with me. They all have my phone number and my email address. Have any of your friends besides Jenna called or emailed you? I haven't heard from any of them."

She said nothing.

"They don't love you or care about you. If they did, they'd have called. They'd have wondered where you are and how you're doing."

She twisted to the side, to put her back to me.

"Do you know who loves you? I do. Your Dad does. Your family does."

Tears of anger and sadness and frustration poured down my cheeks.

"Do you think I'm homeschooling you because it's so much fun for me? Because I had too much free time on my hands and needed something to do? I gave up my life to do this. Why? Because I love you. Because I think that public school was destructive for you. I'm doing this because I will do anything to keep you safe and healthy, and to give you the best possible chance for a healthy and happy future."

I wept, silently pleading the same mantra I'd been praying for over a year: I want my daughter back!

"Those people at school do not care about you. But I love you. I will never leave you and I will never give up on you. I will never

quit trying to do the very best I can for you, even when you hate me for it."

I'd said more than I probably should have. But I needed to say it. I needed her to hear it.

I got up and went back inside.

She didn't come in.

When the day ended, she followed her sister and me to the car without a word.

But the next day everything changed.

Emma did her work for homeschool with a fairly good attitude. Although she maintained for the rest of the year that she didn't like homeschool, working with her no longer felt like trying to pull a sitting donkey uphill through the mud.

Both the homeschool community director and Emma's therapist told me the same thing about the day Emma refused to go to class: "That was her final, all-in, throw-down attempt to get you to give up and let her have her way. When you didn't cave, she gave in and turned it around."

The rest of the year wasn't all starlight, ponies, and roses, but we made it through.

And I'd do the same thing again in a heartbeat.

Emma has since desisted from the transgender narrative. Her mother said it took about another year after that pivotal day.

Special Considerations: Young Children, Adolescents/Teens, and Young Adults

Keep your ultimate goal in mind as you pursue conversations with your child: *you want your child to leave the gender cult and accept his or her birth sex as reality.* In order for that to happen, your child must trust that you and home are a soft landing place. Constantly ask yourself, "Is what I'm about to do or say likely to bring my child closer to me and to home, or to push my child farther away from me and from home?" Although conversations should challenge the child's logic, they should never make the child feel belittled, intimidated, or afraid of you. Your child must know that your love is unconditional and trustworthy, so much so that you will not consent or capitulate to harmful or untruthful pursuits.

YOUNG CHILDREN

Prepubescent children (up to about age twelve) tend to be strongly identified with the family and take direction from family values and culture, provided the home has been a healthy environment and the child is generally emotionally and psychologically healthy.[67]

Very young children (up to roughly age nine) may have robust fantasy lives. Some children create imaginary friends as well as complex alternate realities. Evidence of the child's developing imagination, these role-playing activities are usually a normal activity.[68]

If a very young child claims an alternate sex identity (e.g., a four-year-old boy says he's a girl) this is likely just role-play, no different from a child who says he's a cowboy, an astronaut, or a T. rex. Simply respond, "Oh, that's interesting. It's fun to try being different people, isn't it?" and indulge the child's imaginary play. If the role-play continues persistently for a long time (maybe more than a week or two) and is accompanied by other concerning issues, such as a major life change for the child (parents' divorce, birth or death of a sibling, a traumatic move), it might be wise to consult a trusted mental-healthcare professional to make sure there's nothing else going on. (See chapter 6 for a discussion about finding a trustworthy therapist.)

Pediatrician Michelle Cretella tells of a young patient who suddenly insisted he was a girl. Dr. Cretella referred Andy and his family to a reputable counselor who helped the boy articulate what was really going on. Andy's little sister had been born with special needs, redirecting much of his parents' attention — which had previously been all Andy's — onto caring for his sister's needs. Andy interpreted this shift of attention as evidence that his parents liked girls more than boys. He deduced that in order to get his parents' love back, he needed to be a girl. With the counselor's help, the family addressed Andy's errant understanding and assured him of their love. He happily returned to identifying as a boy.[69]

If your young child persists in identifying as an alternate sex, take care that your conversations around sex-related issues are developmentally appropriate. Use accurate words and phrases, but keep them at a level that the child can understand. A typical five-year-old can understand the terms *penis* and *vagina*, for example, but may get lost in a discussion that includes terms like *sex gametes* and *male/female reproductive organs*. Young children may have learned a wide variety of gender-industry terms at school, but may not really grasp what they mean, or may have a mistaken understanding of their definitions. It is neither normal nor developmentally appropriate for prepubescent children to have a driving interest in or extensive knowledge of sexual relationships.[70]

Ask open-ended questions, listen to the answers, and correct young children's flawed understanding with compassion and respect.

ADOLESCENTS/TEENS

From about age twelve, children start to focus more on their friendships and relationships outside the home. This does not mean that home and family are less important. But children have now moved into the later stages of their brain development, where they can process abstract ideas; reason logically about moral, political, and philosophical concepts;[71] and interact with the world with less oversight from their parents. They still need (and want, though they often insist otherwise) the firm foundation of their parents' home and protection to guide them as they start to move toward independence.

Parent-child relationships are often at their most strained during this tenuous season when children are still minors but want very much to be adults who are the captains of their own destinies. Your child may demand that you get out of her life and stop trying to control her, ten minutes before she collapses in a sobbing breakdown because her favorite shirt is dirty, and can you wash it for her and then make her a cup of hot cocoa, and put those little marshmallows in it, please?

One helpful strategy when having difficult conversations with tweens and teens can be to pass a journal or notebook back and forth. If face-to-face discussions are repeatedly proving awkward, strained, or unproductive, writing letters to each other in a journal (or even via email) can be a lifesaver. Letter-writing also provides the opportunity for you both to give deep thought to what you want to say before you respond to the other, to prevent you from saying something in the heat of the moment that you later wish you hadn't.

These five other relationship tweaks may also smooth over some of the rough spots with your adolescent:

1. **Make Your First Interactions Positive**

   When greeting your child first thing in the morning, after returning home from school/work, or following any kind of separation, make the first words you say *positive* ones.

   "Good morning. How did you sleep?" is good; "Why didn't you put the trash out at the curb like I told you to last night?" is not so good.

"Glad you're home. How was your day?" is warm and welcoming; "I'll bet you left your math textbook at school again, didn't you?" not so much.

"Getting some R and R?" is a nonjudgmental comment that recognizes the value of down time; "Have you done anything today other than lie on the couch playing video games?" will throw a kid into defensive mode faster than chucking an angry raccoon at his head.

If, upon reconnecting with your child after a separation, your initial opener is consistently negative, your child will quickly learn to dread the sight of you. How would you feel if every morning when you walked into work, your boss met you at the door with a demand or a criticism?

The very first moment you reconnect with your child after a separation is not the right time to battle the gender cult or engage in disciplinary training. Create a caring, positive atmosphere first.

2. **Ask Open-Ended Questions**

Older kids are notoriously noncommunicative. Whereas five or ten years ago we'd gladly have paid half a month's salary to get them to be quiet for an hour, now an invisible switch has flipped. "Fine," "Yes," and "No" comprise the complete and universal teenager responses to any questions for which those answers will suffice, such as:

"How was your day?"

"Is everything okay?"

"Did anything exciting happen?"

We may feel that if we don't ask these questions we will never again hear the voices of our offspring, but this isn't true.

(We'll talk more about the remarkable value of adult silence in the next section.) But let's look at how the way we word our questions can change the responses we get.

Closed questions, like those above, typically get a binary (yes/no) or single-word response. Open-ended questions (like those beginning with *Who, What, When, Where, Why,* and *How*) can't usually be answered so dismissively.

"What did your teacher say about your history project?"

"How are you handling that problem with Brian?"

"Tell me what you're enjoying and what you're not enjoying about tenth grade so far."

Open-ended questions not only elicit deeper answers, but they also communicate deeper understanding and greater interest from the person who asked. Hard as it may be to believe, our kids actually do want to talk to us. And when we give them reasons to think that we're interested in them and in their world, they'll open up.

Which brings us to the surprising benefits of shutting up.

3. **Listen 80/Speak 20**

Parents need to get comfortable with silence, because if *we're* talking, we're taking up space in which *our kids* could be talking. Time is a finite thing; what I use leaves less for you.

A good benchmark to strive toward with teens is for parents to listen 80 percent of the time and talk 20 percent. This is admittedly difficult. We've been in teach-instruct-train mode with our children for so long, it's hard to change gears. But by this stage of the game our kids know what we think about pretty much everything. They've been listening, observing, and absorbing our guidance, knowledge, and wisdom for over a dozen years. They know where we stand on most issues.

During this season of their lives, they're trying to figure out whether they agree with us or not.

So when a kid says, "I heard that a guy in my class has been smoking weed," this is exactly the wrong time for the parent to launch into a lecture about the dangers and horrors of drug use. That kid already knows that Dad either wants him to stay a hundred miles away from the druggies, or that Dad hopes the classmate might hook him up with some ganja.

The parent and the parent's perspective are not the subject of the conversation. The *child* and the *child's perspective* are.

What's a better adult response? "What do you think about that?"

Then we shut up and listen. (And ask open-ended questions judiciously.)

4. **Praise What They Do, Not Who They Are**

As we mentioned earlier, people perform better when they're praised for traits over which they have control than if they're praised for qualities they feel are innate and fixed.

For example, kids who hear, "You succeeded because you worked really hard," tend to try even harder when challenges arise. They believe that success is a function of perseverance. On the other hand, kids who are told, "You succeeded because you're so smart," exhibit the opposite behavior. They give up more easily when confronted with an obstacle, because they fear that failure will prove they aren't as smart as others think they are.[72]

When a kid pats himself on the back for how brilliant he is, we can say, "Yeah, you're a pretty smart cookie. But what impressed me was how much time and effort you put into that science fair project." Conversely, if he claims he's dumb, we can counter with, "I don't think that at all and I hope you don't think that about yourself. But regardless, you showed by that song you wrote what great work you can do when you put your mind to something."

5. **In Moments of Crisis Don't Tell Them What to Do, But Ask Them What They Need**

Lastly, we have to quit being our kids' problem solvers. This one's really hard too, both because we've been putting out all the fires for so long and because we've gotten pretty good at managing disasters. When the poo hits the fan, I can probably stop the carnage and clean it up a lot faster and more efficiently than my kids can.

But in order to become functional adults, our children must learn to deal with their own crises. What better time than now to learn those skills, while they still have an adult nearby to back them up?

When the child realizes, as the bus is coming down the street, that he never packed his lunch, resist the temptation to

a) throw some grub in a bag for him on the way out the door,

b) stuff a fiver in his pocket to buy lunch, or

c) lament his failures as you chase him across the street with a banana and a granola bar.

Instead, just say, "How can I help?"

When she calls from school to say she forgot her homework: "How are you going to resolve this?"

When your children tear the seam of a new garment they were fighting over, just minutes before you need to walk out the door: "Whether you two are dressed or not, we're leaving in ten minutes. Figure it out."

Giving them ownership in resolving a problem shows we respect and have confidence in their abilities. And it's pretty amazing how kids can step up when we get out of the way.

YOUNG ADULTS

Older kids — and especially those who are eighteen and over — are a different ball game. Unfortunately, you don't have as much influence over them, unless they're living at home and/or you're paying the bills. And the fact is, if you cut off the funding, they're likely to cut you off in return. Transgender-identified people today have no shortage of glitter families and financial support from gender-industry groomers. It's harder to have consistent, strategic conversations if your child is no longer in your circle.

But don't give up. Keep making overtures that demonstrate that you love your child:

Send birthday and Christmas gifts.

Send small gifts or cards on minor holidays, or just to say, "I'm thinking about you."

Text occasionally with a question, a joke, or just to ask how things are. (Don't text every day, or even every week, if your relationship is especially strained. You want to be perceived as a steadfast friend, not a stalker or a pest.)

Invite your child to family events, even if you never get a response. Someday you might.

Ask if you can take him or her out for lunch or dinner.

Ask your child for a favor. (Remember the *Benjamin Franklin effect* we talked about in chapter 2.)

Do not, however, let yourself be manipulated. Remember the boundaries you set and maintain those unless a compelling reason arises for you to reconsider them. The gender industry teaches its recruits how to emotionally manipulate others to get what they want. But "No" is not a four-letter word, and refusing to do something you don't feel right about is not tantamount to committing an atrocity.

Throughout history people have survived true horrors like enslavement, prison camps, torture, traumatic injuries, chronic illnesses, despotic government brutality, and long-term abuse. However:

- being *misgendered,* or hearing one's unpreferred, parent-bestowed name spoken aloud is not an "act of violence,"[73] but merely an irritation.
- disagreement or disapproval from others represents neither oppression nor persecution, although it may spark disappointment.
- using emotional or political manipulation to coerce others to do what you want them to do is not kind, just, or tolerant; it is dictatorial, autocratic, and small-minded.

Focus Always on the Goal

The journey with a transgender-identified child can be prolonged, exhausting, and demoralizing. Cult indoctrination subverts a person's true identity and imposes a cult identity that is vigorously maintained through the mind-control techniques discussed in chapter 1. In many ways, you are not dealing with your child, but with a puppet that the gender industry has put onto your child, like a costume he or she can't take off, with someone else's script dictating every word.

Your goal is to bring your child back into alignment with reality, and back into allegiance with your family, and to accept the identity of his or her sexed body. You're trying to help your child take off the costume and find his or her own voice again.

People usually end up where they feel most loved and valued. If your child has been sucked into the transgender community, it is because the ideology serves some need that has not been fulfilled elsewhere. In the next chapter we'll uncover some of the reasons why kids may be susceptible to gender ideology, as well as discuss a strategy for pulling a child out of the gender cult.

CHAPTER 4

A Plan for Deprogramming Transgender-Identified Children

"Being away from people who affirmed made all the difference. Working on the relationship with sympathy and validation also made all the difference. Never affirmed."

— Mother of a desister

WHEN YOU HEAR THE word *deprogramming,* you may imagine a team of Navy SEAL-like infiltrators sneaking into a fortified compound at night to kidnap a cult member and deliver him kicking and screaming to a forced intervention. That's not far off from what used to happen when family members or friends believed someone had been brainwashed into a cult.

But today the gender cult has permeated nearly every corner of society. Your child may have entered the "cult compound" at school, within a community or friend group, or from inside your own home, via endless transgender-themed rabbit holes on Tumblr, Reddit, and other myriad, unmediated social media platforms.

It's nearly impossible to physically abduct a child away from this cult, because the cult's influence and henchmen are everywhere: they've taken over social media, schools, the marketplace, the entertainment industry, and even many churches.

Furthermore, while involuntary deprogramming may have had some limited success, better, more ethical, and ultimately more successful methods may exist. In this chapter we'll look at a potential strategy for pulling children out of the gender cult. By combining long-understood principles of child development and psychology with lessons learned from families who have successfully gotten their children back from this insidious ideology, we'll do three things:

1. Figure out what happened.

2. Sort out the protagonists and the antagonists.

3. Undertake a campaign to undo the effects of gender brainwashing.

Figure Out What Happened

Each child is unique, and while the gender cult imposes on its victims a very recognizable and almost clichéd pattern of behaviors and beliefs, it's important not only to consider what the child believes about the cult and its ideology, but also to understand a number of other aspects of the child's individual situation:

✣ What about this child's psychology or life experience created a vulnerability to the gender cult? What unmet need is the cult fulfilling?

✣ What are the facts versus what does the child believe about his or her identity, life, and family?

✣ Who is currently influencing the child and what mind control techniques are being applied to maintain the child's allegiance to the cult?

WHY MIGHT A CHILD ADOPT A FALSE IDENTITY?

As we look at a wide variety of reasons why a child might be susceptible to cult indoctrination, the primary motivator in nearly every one of these cases is the same:

The gender industry tells people that they feel unhappy/uncomfortable/in pain because their minds and bodies are mismatched and they require medical alteration.

In every situation below we will see that this lie is proffered as a panacea that will supposedly fix anything and everything. Kids who claim a transgender identity are very often trying to escape some kind of pain. Children are told, "You will feel better after you transition sexes." But the burgeoning ranks of detransitioners tell us otherwise.[74]

A 2018 study by Lisa Littman of Brown University (which was met with such hostility by the gender industry that Brown temporarily unpublished the work and ordered a post-publication reassessment before releasing it again[75]) found that 62.5 percent of the 256 subjects presented with a diagnosed mental health or neurological disorder prior to adopting a transgender identity.[76] It is not unreasonable to assume that some portion of the other 37.5 percent also suffered such issues but had not yet been officially diagnosed.

Autism Spectrum Disorder[77]

A 2019 study published in the journal *European Psychiatry* found that 14 percent of those who identify as transgender had an autism diagnosis while an additional 28 percent (42 percent of the subjects in total) met criteria for an autism diagnosis, although they had not yet received an official diagnosis.[78] According to the Centers for Disease Control, the prevalence of autism in the general population is between 2 to 3 percent[79]; seeing that number multiplied *five to ten times* in the transgender-identified population should be a clear and obvious red flag that something else may be going on besides sex confusion.

Autistic people present with a variety of neurological differences, such as sensory integration issues, difficulties understanding social cues, rigid black-and-white thinking, discomfort with changes in routine or expectations, and perseveration (hyperfocus, or getting "stuck" on a topic or activity of interest), among other issues. These symptoms suggest a number of possible explanations why autistic children might be vulnerable to the deceptive message, "You are uncomfortable because you are transgender"[80]:

✠ Many autistic people experience varying levels of discomfort with their own bodies because of sensory integration issues. Feeling physically uncomfortable with themselves may prompt them to seek both a diagnosis (if they are unaware that they are on the autism spectrum, or unaware of this particular facet of autism) and a remedy. Transgender ideology (falsely) offers both. Additionally, weighted blankets and compression garments have proven comforting to many people on the autism spectrum, alleviating symptoms such as insomnia, anxiety, and irritability. A compelling theory suggests that chest binders may appeal to autistic girls because of the compression they provide.

✢ People on the autism spectrum recognize that they are different from neurotypical (non-autistic) people, and that their traits and behaviors often set them apart socially.[81] They don't feel like they fit into any social groups. One autistic girl (now desisted) reported, "I didn't have a friend group until I joined the GSA club. Then I had a lot of friends. When I said I thought I was transgender, I was suddenly cool and popular."

✢ Black-and-white thinking — a hallmark of autism — makes it very difficult for an autistic person to change his or her mind after settling on a decision. This all-or-nothing rigidity also lends itself to accepting the gender industry's stereotype-based ideology: "If I don't think I fit in perfectly with my sex category (male or female) then that means I am in the opposite sex category (or perhaps no sex category)."[82]

✢ Changes can cause intense distress to people on the autism spectrum[83]; they are known to struggle during times of transition, such as when a teacher says, "Put away your math text and take out your English notebook." At no other time in one's life are bigger changes taking place than during puberty: physical, emotional, intellectual, and social developments can feel like an ongoing natural disaster to the most typical and stable of children. For autism spectrum kids, puberty can be much more than a crisis; it may feel like a cataclysm. But instead of being told that their distress is normal and will abate with time, they are instead told that they are suffering because they are in the wrong bodies. This heinous lie is nothing short of abuse.

✢ Autistic people develop fixations on things and ideas, which may last weeks, months, or years, and they will explore everything about their interest until they have exhausted its study.[84] One therapist told a parent of a transgender-identified child (who later desisted), "Transgenderism is your child's obsession right now. You're just going to have to hang on until this runs its course and she moves on to a different interest."

Any child who is suspected to have autism spectrum disorder should be fully screened for that diagnosis before a transgender self-identification is pursued. The transgender self-identification of a child who already has an autism diagnosis must be extremely suspect. At the very least, every other autism-related explanation should be considered. In addition, the typical time period during which the individual tends to perseverate on special interests (weeks, months, or years) should pass before one can state with any degree of certainty that the transgender-identification is not simply an autism-related fixated interest.[85]

Trauma[86]

A significant number of transgender-identified children present with traumatic experiences in their personal histories. Some sources of trauma include parental divorce or abuse, the birth or death of a sibling, death of or separation from a loved one, a significant life change such as a move or a traumatic injury, or ongoing rejection or bullying.

Sexual abuse seems to be a common precursor to asserting a transgender identity, as a child may blame his or her body for the assault and mistakenly deduce that were his or her body the opposite sex such abuse wouldn't have happened (and won't happen again).[87]

Children who have been profoundly traumatized (via sexual or any other kind of abuse) may dissociate from their bodies as a coping strategy. Dissociation occurs when the mind disconnects from the body in order to distance itself from what is happening. People who have developed dissociative disorders sometimes describe the experience as though they are watching events that are happening to someone else. Dissociation affects memory, identity, emotion, perception, behavior, and one's sense of self.[88]

Transgender ideology settles seamlessly on top of a person who's dealing with trauma; it encourages dissociation instead of healing. The possibility that one can escape his or her body and/or past offers a tremendous amount of (false) hope.

Depression[89]

Depression and anxiety commonly co-occur with a transgender self-identification, perhaps because these two mental health issues are so prevalent in society today, especially among young people. Depression among teenagers rose 59 percent in the decade between 2007 and 2017, according to a Pew Research Center report.[90]

The possible reasons for this troubling increase are outside the scope of this book, but should certainly be considered if a transgender-identified person also presents with depression or anxiety. A competent and trustworthy therapist should investigate and treat a transgender person's mental health issues, such as depression, before ever suggesting or supporting medical interventions for gender dysphoria or transgender identification.

Transgender-rights activists claim that transgender-identified people suffer adverse mental health outcomes like depression and anxiety because of society's bigotry against and oppression of them, but such assertions have questionable credibility. It may be equally likely that depression leads to gender dysphoria, or that some third factor — whether cultural trends or a strategic marketing campaign to recruit young people into transgender ideology —

is causing concurrent escalations in both depression and transgender identification.

If a child has been medicated for depression (or any other mental health issue), it is important to recognize that the side effects of certain medications may instigate or increase feelings that lead a child to question his or her sexuality or personhood. It is well-known that some antidepressants, for example, can diminish libido. For a young person who may be entering or passing through puberty, lack of sexual interest may be grounds for questioning his or her sexuality and/or gender identity. Unfortunately, little research exists on the effects of psychiatric drugs on one's sense of sex or gender.

Other Mental Health Struggles

People who suffer gender dysphoria and/or identify as transgender frequently present with a number of other mental health issues, including attention-deficit disorder, self-harming behaviors such as self-cutting, eating disorders, mood disorders, psychotic disorders, suicidal ideation, and attempts at suicide.[91]

Again, the transgender activism community insists that such disorders are a result of society's maltreatment of transgender-identified people, and these political idealogues will brook no discussion of any other possible explanations. But even in the most LGB- and TQ-friendly countries such as Sweden,[92] similar trends prevail, underscoring the likelihood that underlying mental health issues tend to drive an individual's transgender identification, rather than the other way around.

No matter what the reasons for the co-occurrence of transgender-identification and mental health disorders, in any case where a transgender-identified person wishes to undertake medical transition (use of puberty blockers, wrong-sex hormones, and/or surgeries) the mental health issue(s) must first be resolved. Common sense alone tells us that a person who is struggling with any kind of mental health disorder is not, by definition, capable of making reasonable and informed decisions regarding major life choices. His or her psychological state must first be put to rights before any treatment for transgender identification is pursued.

The transgender-identified person may claim that "fixing" the body will also fix the mind. But as we've seen from detransitioners and emerging research, such claims are not supported.[93] The fact that the transgender-identified person is suffering from a mental health disorder should immediately make his or her judgment (pertaining to major, permanent decisions) suspect until that disorder is resolved.

Social Contagion

In addition to a preponderance of mental health issues, Littman's Brown University study also uncovered compelling evidence that the staggering explosion of transgender identification among youth may be attributable to social influence:

> The expected prevalence of transgender young adult individuals is 0.7%. Yet, according to the parental reports, more than a third of the friendship groups described in this study had 50% or more of the [adolescents and young adults] in the group becoming transgender-identified in a similar time frame. This suggests a localized increase to more than 70 times the expected prevalence rate.[94]

That kids are "coming out" in friend groups is undeniable. Detransitioners like the four young women of the Pique Resilience Project describe in detail how interactions in friend groups spurred them on in their desire to transition out of their birth sex category.[95]

But a more insidious and intentional agenda utilizes peer pressure to indoctrinate kids into gender ideology. Transgender-identified kids from high schools' GSA clubs now teach about sex and gender ideology in health, physical education, and other classes during the school day.[96]

The business world's billion-dollar peer-to-peer sales model,[97] which has generated an industry of social media influencers, has been adopted by the National Education Association (NEA) and renamed "Peer-Led Sex Ed."[98]

"Having a peer teach them about sex has the ability to be able to speak to them on their level."[99] Yes, but having a peer teach sex education also has the ability to create enormous peer pressure.

Peer-Led Sex Ed "teachers" get their credentials simply by joining a GSA (a.k.a. Equality or Spectrum) club. GSAs are touted as support groups for LGB and TQ kids. Promoted and funded by the NEA, Planned Parenthood, and the Human Rights Campaign,[100] GSA clubs are actually boots-on-the-ground for indoctrinating kids into gender ideology. These clubs are central to the cult's strategy of recruitment, love-bombing, and inculcation of the beliefs and behaviors demanded by the gender industry.

The NEA is so committed to indoctrinating kids into gender ideology that it offers financial incentives for teachers and counselors who do so. Rebecca Friedrichs, a twenty-eight-year veteran teacher, describes NEA conferences promoting GSA formation. "If you agreed to start a [GSA] … you could get big money.… You could also get money to push LGBT activism in the classroom."[101]

All topics related to human sexuality are supposed to be housed under schools' Family Life Education (FLE) programs, and parents' right to opt their children out of FLE is legally protected in most states in the United States. But by fallaciously claiming that transgender ideology is a civil rights issue, sex and gender ideology are now taught throughout school curriculum and in any and all subject areas.[102]

Given the current state of public schools and their aggressive promotion of gender ideology, it may be unwise for any parent to place any child in a public school in the United States (and many other countries), much less a child who presents with a transgender identity.

Pornography

Today's culture is saturated with pornography and sexual messaging. Ninety-two percent of Billboard's top 10 hits are about sex.[103] Sex and sexism permeate advertising.[104] When the TV sitcom *I Love Lucy* ran in the 1960s, even two people who were married (both on the program and in real life) had to be shown in separate twin beds if a bedroom scene took place; today, however, PG-13 movies are allowed "brief nudity"[105] and couples frequently end up in bed on screen after their first date (or before).

Fifty percent of children ages eleven to thirteen have viewed pornography. That number increases to 78 percent by age seventeen. Girls report having watched porn in order to meet boys' expectations of them. Pornhub's daily visits now exceed one hundred million, and every minute 63,992 *new visitors* come to the site.[106]

Pornography has not only become more pervasive in recent years, it's also become more brutal.[107] Porn:

- ✠ teaches that women enjoy violent sex. Thirty-eight percent of women under the age of forty report having experienced unwanted slapping, gagging, choking, and spitting during sex.

- portrays paraphilias (e.g., sex with animals or children, sex that involves excrement) and rape.
- increases the likelihood that users will commit sexual offenses.
- increases female victimization and trafficking of women and children for sexual use.
- leads significant numbers of viewers to purchase sex, and these buyers report their sexual preferences having altered so they craved more sadistic and masochistic experiences.

Given these statistics, it should not be a surprise that boys and men have been sexually pathologized by the porn industry. Porn use has been linked to erectile dysfunction, inability to perform sexually with a real person, and less satisfaction with sex.[108]

It seems reasonable to consider that pornography may, at least in part, be fueling the rise of transgender-identification as well.

Historically, almost all transsexuals were adult men. They fell into two categories: homosexuals who were ashamed of their sexual orientation and therefore rationalized that they were actually meant to be women, and autogynephiles. *Autogynephilia* is a paraphilia (disorder of sexual desire) wherein a male is sexually aroused by presenting himself or seeing himself as a female.[109]

In some cases (but certainly not all) where men or boys adopt a transgender identification, either a guilt response to a homosexual orientation or autogynephilia may be the root cause. Porn consumption may be a launching pad particularly for autogynephilia.[110]

For girls and women, exposure to pornography may cause them to want to opt out of womanhood altogether. In a review of Abigail Shrier's *Irreversible Damage*, Jean C. Lloyd explains:

Shrier exposes a multi-faceted, full-blown crisis for girls of this generation. They are lonelier, less valued, and increasingly depressed. Life is more online and less in person than ever, and social media, their main connection to others, is an instrument of angst — a megaphone and microscope that amplifies and exposes their (and others') every flaw. Violence in pornography is ubiquitous; the girls are not unaware and are rightly frightened. Consider the horrifying practice of choking during sexual activity — now the porn *du jour*, and which a full 13 percent of sexually active girls ages 14 to 17 report having already experienced....

... Girls today "flee womanhood like a house on fire, their minds fixed on escape, not on any particular destination." Cue the siren call of transition, beckoning over the internet and media waves, with doctors and therapists standing ready to encourage — and profit. According to Sasha Ayad, who works exclusively with gender-dysphoric adolescents, many of her clients are unsure they want to be boys, they only know they don't want to be girls.[111]

Facts vs. Fiction: What Is Real, What Is Being Taught, and What Is Believed?

Before effectively convincing your child that what he or she believes about sex and personhood is in error, you must first determine what you believe to be true about the issues. Our present discussion here is informed by the following understandings:

SEX IS BINARY.[112]

Humans, like all mammals, come in only two varieties (male and female) with respect to their ability to produce young. This distinction is based upon what kind of sex organs a person has. Female bodies produce eggs and male bodies produce sperm. Both of those two gametes are necessary to create life. No third type of non-disordered human is required, or exists.

DISORDER DOES NOT EQUAL DIVERSITY.[113]

During conception or gestation something occasionally goes wrong and a child is born with a birth defect. This can result in chromosomal disorders, like Down's syndrome or Klinefelter syndrome. A very small percentage of people are born with a *disorder of sexual development*, also called being *intersex*, where it's not immediately clear whether the person is male or female. By looking at these people's anatomy, sex glands, and DNA, it's almost always obvious what nature intended before something went awry. "Intersex" conditions are evidence not of diversity (also wrongly called a *gender spectrum*) but of something gone wrong during conception or gestation.

GENDER IS MEANINGLESS.

See chapter one.

EVERY CHILD IS BORN IN THE RIGHT BODY.

There are male bodies and female bodies. Some claim that one's mind, spirit, or soul can have a gender (a meaningless concept based on stereotypes) that is different from one's body. This is not supported by science. One's mind, spirit, or soul contains (or expresses) one's personality, and personality comes in a wide variety of diverse types, none of which must conform to stereotypes about masculinity or femininity.

Your body is you.

People who say that a person can be "born in the wrong body" believe that the mind is separate from (and more important than) the body. They believe that when people do not feel comfortable with their sex, they should change their bodies. Not only is this impossible (people cannot change sex), but it is also a lie that a person's body is completely separate from that person's mind. Body and mind are two parts of the same thing: a whole, integrated person.

People cannot change sex.[114]

Until very recently, when people experienced *gender dysphoria*, which means they don't feel comfortable with the sex (maleness or femaleness) of their body, therapists tried to help them heal their minds so that they could accept their bodies. Today some therapists say it is easier to change the body than to change the mind. But that is untrue. Sex is written into every cell of the body. Men's and women's genes are different, their organs are different, and their body structure is different. Taking opposite-sex hormones or surgically changing the body by cutting off or adding parts to it does not change one's sex. It only helps a person pretend to be the other sex. Pretending to be something one is not is unhealthy for both the body and the mind.

Everyone deserves dignity.

We are all broken people in one way or another. Every one of us has something that needs to be healed, whether in our minds or in our bodies. People who experience gender dysphoria should be treated with kindness and respect just as much as someone who is missing an arm, or who suffers from depression, or who doesn't seem to have anything wrong at all. All people deserve dignity.

TRUTH IS NOT HATE.

Some people say that it is unkind to disagree with someone else's feelings or thoughts. Some believe that feelings or thoughts are more real than the physical world. But neither is true. Feelings and thoughts can mislead. Anorexics (people who have a disease that makes them want to starve themselves) actually believe when looking in the mirror that they are fat, even though their bodies may be little more than skin and bones. Their minds are ill and can't see reality. We would never agree that it is kind to tell an anorexic, "Yes, you really are fat. You should keep dieting." The anorexic will die if starvation continues. In the same way, it is not hateful to tell a gender dysphoric person that he or she was born in exactly the right body.

FEELINGS ARE NOT FACTS.

Feelings exist to either tell us that something is good and we should try to get more of it (as when we fall in love) or that something is wrong and we need to do something to fix it (as when someone hurts us). Feelings can mislead, such as when we get angry because we see the person we love hug someone else and we think he is being unfaithful. But when we learn the truth — that the person he hugged was just his sister — we discover that our feeling was wrong because it was based on a misunderstanding of the facts. Facts are based in reality. Feelings are based on our perception of reality. Feelings are important, but only because they tell us that we need to deal with reality.

Unfortunately, facts like those above are no longer being taught in many schools. Throughout the culture and the world, lies about sex and personhood have been presented to people as facts. Whole dissertations have been written on various nonsensical themes around one central, flawed premise: that sex is a social construct and gender is on a spectrum. Every other fiction, fabrication, and deceit around gender ideology rolls out from this principal perversion of fact.

Sex is not a social construct; sex is a binary based on observable, immutable, biological fact. Gender, on the other hand, is a social construct based entirely on regressive sex-based stereotypes (see chapter one).

Two of the most common lies taught by gender-industry activists, especially to young children, are that "One can be born in the wrong body,"[115] and that "God made a mistake."[116] Although we have already discussed arguments that defeat the first lie, the second lie can similarly be dismantled by investigating the only three corollaries that can flow out of the idea that God might err: (1) God is cruel; (2) God is incompetent; or (3) God doesn't exist.

GOD IS CRUEL

One of the claims that transgender rights activists frequently make to support belief in a gender spectrum (infinite genders), as opposed to a binary (male and female), is diversity. They argue that gender is like skin color or like the variety of animal species in nature. They assert that God — if they address God at all — isn't a limited or limiting god, but a god who celebrates diversity in every aspect of his creation.

However, if God is sovereign and omnipotent (all-powerful) *and* God intentionally creates persons whose inner landscape (their "gender") is mismatched to their outer landscape (their physical sex), then we can only conclude that God is cruel. To specifically design a creature whose mind and body are at odds with one another is to create a lack of integrity (here meaning integrated-ness, or symbiosis of the system), which must by definition cause the creature pain and suffering.

The transgender narrative explains this pain and suffering as being a result of societal nonacceptance. But no matter what one experiences at the hands of others, certainly the very state of existing at war with oneself creates its own inherent pain and lack of peace. To believe that God would deliberately curse someone to live in disharmony with himself, or be required to undergo extensive and lifelong medicalization through human-handed surgery and drug treatment in an attempt to achieve harmony, is to paint God as a sadist.

GOD IS INCOMPETENT

Most religious holy texts are clear on three points about their deity: God is omnipotent (all-powerful), God is omniscient (all-knowing), and God is omnipresent (all-seeing). Biblical references to these three characteristics include:

> "Ah, Sovereign LORD, you have made the heavens and the earth by your great power and outstretched arm. Nothing is too hard for you." (Jer. 32:17)
>
> "Who can fathom the Spirit of the LORD, or instruct the LORD as his counselor? Whom did the LORD consult to enlighten him, and who taught him the right way? Who was it that taught him knowledge, or showed him the path of understanding?" (Isa. 40:13–14)
>
> "Where can I go from your Spirit? Where can I flee from your presence?" (Ps. 139:7)

To claim that God can err is to negate God's power, perfection, and/or perception. We may rightly claim that sin has corrupted all of creation via man's will to exalt himself as his own god, but to believe that God lacks the power, wisdom, or attentiveness to initiate creation without flaw is to try to bring God down to man's level.

If a person believes that God is incompetent, that person does not subscribe to the most basic tenets of most faith traditions.

THERE IS NO GOD

This is the only theological position in support of transgender ideology that is intellectually honest.

If I do not believe in a primary creator and ultimate authority over that creation, I am free to be and do anything I want. This anti-theology is at the very heart of the transgender narrative: people are nothing but clay that can mold itself into any shape it desires. The clay was made by no one, has no meaning to its existence other than self-satisfaction, and owes nothing to anyone or anything outside itself.

The atheist position on transgender rights is the only one that holds water, because its argument derives from the genuine belief that there is no such thing as ultimate truth. When working from that foundation (or lack of a foundation), transgender ideology is the logical conclusion to the question "What is the sexual purpose of humankind?" The atheist's answer: "Its own happiness." Without the constraints of any kind of theology, nothing more can be required of a life than self-actualization.

But for someone who claims faith in one of most traditional theologies, affirming transgender ideology as acceptable requires denial of one's own beliefs. It underscores a greater desire for self-satisfaction and/or approval from others than for approval from God. It points to the elevation of the self as its own god, and the relegation of God to irrelevance.

In the case of transgender ideology, one is either for God or against God. Trying to ride the fence only drops a person on the latter side, no matter how passionately he claims the former.

In addition to lies about biological and theological facts that have been inculcated in gender cult members, transgender-identified people very often rewrite their own histories as well, to better fit the narrative with which the cult wants them to align. Cult members may be asked about their families, and then any negative experiences or emotions are highlighted and emphasized while positive events and feelings are downplayed, as described in this excerpt from *Cults in Our Midst*:

> Cults have been leading followers to create revised histories for some years now. Members have been made to gradually accuse parents and family and separate from them, then they are repeatedly rewarded for these actions and statements.... Many times, former cult members will have written hateful, accusatory letters — the so-called disconnect letters — to parents and relatives at the direction of the cult after they were led to believe that their parents acted in accordance with the fabrications concocted during history revision.[117]

If your child insists that certain events happened, of which you have no memory, use the communication techniques discussed in chapters 2 and 3 to address the claims respectfully but truthfully:

✠ "I don't remember that ever happening."

✠ "My memory of that event is quite different. Here's how I remember it."

✠ "I'd like to get your sister's (mother's, friend's, etc.) take on this, since she was there too. Maybe you and I are both remembering that wrong."

If neglect, abuse, or other harm did take place, it's critical that you admit it, apologize for it, and ask your child's forgiveness. By doing so, you honor the truth, show respect for your child, and attempt to restore a break in your relationship. If the event was not a one-off but demonstrates a recurring theme in your behavior, you should seek the help of a trustworthy mental health professional. By working on your own issues, you model the very behavior you're hoping to lead your child through: pursuing truth with the goal of achieving physical, psychological, and relational health.

Determine What Influences and Mind-Control Techniques Are at Work on Your Child

Partners for Ethical Care undertook a survey of people who desisted/detransitioned (no longer claim a transgender identity). Results indicate that children are being introduced to this ideology largely via the Internet.

But it is also clear that most, if not all, of the social forces around the child are actively encouraging and propagating the ideology.

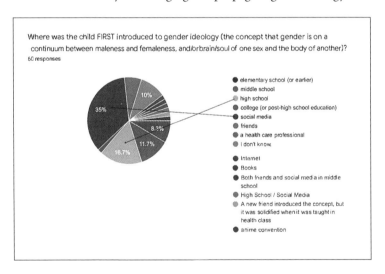

Where was the child FIRST introduced to gender ideology (the concept that gender is on a continuum between maleness and femaleness, and/or brain/soul of one sex and the body of another)?
60 responses

- elementary school (or earlier)
- middle school
- high school
- college (or post-high school education)
- social media
- friends
- a health care professional
- I don't know

- Internet
- Books
- Both friends and social media in middle school
- High School / Social Media
- A new friend introduced the concept, but it was solidified when it was taught in health class
- anime convention

Determining who and what are exerting undue and unhealthy influences on your child is imperative before moving on to the next step of the process, which is building the team that will work with you to get your child back from the gender cult.

Dr. Robert J. Lifton outlines eight ways that cults exert pressure on recruits to create "mind reform," or to bring them in line with cult ideology.[118] Consider where you recognize these tactics at work on your child:

MILIEU CONTROL

This refers to regulation of a person's physical presence. Cults typically isolate members from the rest of society by keeping them sequestered on a compound or in a remote location. Physical separation is less a feature of the gender cult. Because the cult's doctrine has been so successfully integrated into the rest of society, it's unnecessary for the gender industry to bodily segregate cult members.

One does, however, see that cult members are strongly discouraged from considering other points of view, such as visiting websites or reading materials which question or criticize gender ideology. By labeling dissenters as hateful, transphobic, bigoted, and dangerous, the cult prevents its members from interacting with anyone outside their ranks.

MYSTICAL MANIPULATION (PLANNED SPONTANEITY)

In many religious cults, leaders create what appear to be organic, spiritual events in order to persuade the members that God has manifested a physical presence, or that the leaders or cult members have been specifically spoken to or touched by God.

In the gender cult, one worships how one feels at any given moment: whatever one feels inside is given holy status as ultimate truth which cannot be questioned or reasoned with. Nearly any event or experience can be labeled as evidence for one's transgender identification. If a little boy slips his feet into his mother's shoes, the gender cult will reinterpret that behavior as evidence that the boy wants to be a girl. If a teenage girl develops an affinity for baseball caps and hoodies, her style choice is pointed to as a manifestation of her inner masculinity trying to surface. Gender therapist Diane Ehrensaft asserts that if a pre-verbal girl tears a barrette out of her hair, she is sending the gender message that she is really a boy. (One wonders how Ehrensaft would interpret a toddler who puts his socks on his ears, or refuses to wear shoes.)[119]

THE DEMAND FOR PURITY

A sharp and unyielding divide is created between good people and bad people, right thought and wrong thought, moral actions and reprehensible behavior. Those inside the cult are the right, holy, and altruistic community, while those outside are dangerous, immoral, and hateful. This aspect of mind control is particularly effective on people who are black-and-white thinkers, such as those on the autism spectrum.

Anyone who questions anything about the transgender narrative, or who voices any concern about the ideology or about children who are being medicalized as a result of it, is immediately denounced as hateful, bigoted, and phobic, and is very likely to find him- or herself the target of a cancellation campaign. Days before the U.S. House of Representatives was scheduled to vote on the so-called Equality Act (H.R. 5), which substitutes "gender identity" for "(biological) sex" in nondiscrimination law, a large online retailer removed from its shelves a three-year-old scholarly work on transgender ideology's history and harms, with no warning to its author, Ryan Anderson.[120] (Incidentally, the retailer continued to sell Adolf Hitler's *Mein Kampf.*)

CONFESSION

One must confess all wrong actions and thoughts, and repudiate the past self with its wrong views and behaviors. Any missteps must be profusely regretted and atoned for. We see this in spades among the "allies" of the transgender-identified community.

One desister described an event that helped push her out of the gender cult:

> The girl, who at the time identified as a boy, met a group of people who knew her brother. One said to her, "You're George's sister, right?"
>
> She responded, "Yes, but I prefer to be called his brother."
>
> The group apologized extravagantly and at great length for their mistake, assuring the girl that they felt terrible for misgendering her and that it was wonderful that she had discovered her true self and was living authentically.
>
> "It was so ridiculous," the girl recalled. "It was no big deal, and a simple, 'Oh, okay. Sorry about that,' would've been fine. That's what started me thinking that transgenderism is stupid."

SACRED SCIENCE

The belief system is considered inviolable, unquestionable, and without flaw. No questions, concerns, or criticisms are tolerated, from within the group or outside it. When cult members are questioned, they typically parrot thought-stopping slogans or *ad hominem* attacks (e.g., "Transwomen are women!" or "You're a TERF!") that keep them from having to think about what they believe or say.

Loading the Language

All the language around the ideology is taken captive. Words are assigned new meanings (e.g., *affirmation* now means "encouraging someone's self-harming behavior"), new words are created (e.g., "misgendering," "deadname"), and thought-stopping language (e.g., "You're a transphobe") is taught to members in order to prevent them from straying outside the group's doctrine.

Doctrine over Person

Everything in the member's life revolves around the cult belief system. A member's questions about the group's doctrine are deflected and projected back onto the member as problems with the member's intelligence, sanity, or character. Anyone who questions the doctrine is labeled an outsider who is dangerous and must be excised from the community.

We see the *Doctrine over Person* tactic enforced ruthlessly on desisters and detransitioners. As soon as someone goes back to accepting his or her birth sex, the gender cult rejects the person entirely, claims that the person was never really transgender, and frequently bullies and attacks the member personally and publicly. (This behavior contradicts the claim that gender is on a fluid spectrum. Were that really true, then everyone would be included in the "transgender" community, and one could flow either way in the gender-fluid universe: away from one's birth sex or toward it.)

Dispensing of Existence

According to Lifton, "Since the group has an absolute or totalist vision of truth, those who are not in the group are bound up in evil, are not enlightened, are not saved, and do not have the right to exist."[121]

We see this both in the cult's demand that "unsupportive" families be treated as toxic and cut off from the cult member, and in extreme transgender activists and cult members who advocate for violence against and even the death of those who oppose their demands.[122] In 2018 the San Francisco Public Library hosted an exhibit explicitly calling for violence against anti-trans dissenters. The supposed "art exhibit" featured weapons such as baseball bats which could be used to kill TERFs (transgender-exclusive radical feminists), a term which has become a slur used against anyone who doesn't capitulate to the transgender rights agenda.[123]

Having now done the extensive work of assessing your child's situation in terms of what factors made him or her vulnerable to gender ideology, what he or she may believe that is contrary to fact, and how he or she is being controlled by the cult, you can now turn your attention to figuring out who is on your side and who is undermining you with respect to getting your child free of the gender cult.

Sort Out the Protagonists and the Antagonists

You've probably discovered that a great number of people and institutions are working against you if you're trying to get your child out of the gender cult. Schools, healthcare professionals, social media influencers, neighbors, friends, and probably even family members and some clergy have been deluded into the belief that they are saving the child by sabotaging the parents.

But not everyone has sworn allegiance to the trans flag.

Grab a sheet of paper or open up a new document on your device and draw a line down the center to make two columns. Label one column *Protagonists* (people who are on your side) and the other *Antagonists* (those who are working against you). You're going to place the people you know (and those with whom your child has contact) in one of these two columns, or leave them off the sheet altogether if you're not sure where they stand on this issue.

Think about all the social networks to which you belong.

FAMILY

Do the people with whom your child lives support or question the gender cult? Are both parents or primary caregivers in agreement with each other? Are siblings celebrating the child toward sex transition, or are they concerned about the transgender agenda as well? Does the transgender-identified child have particularly close or particularly strained relationships with any members of the nuclear family? Place these people's names in the appropriate columns.

One caveat: do not expect younger children to take an active role toward deprogramming their older sibling, unless they are adults. This experience can be destabilizing and frightening for children, and they need special support for their own needs; they are unlikely to be strong enough to give support "upward" toward their older brother or sister, and asking it of them would be unfairly burdensome. The same may be true of older siblings who are still children themselves. (We'll discuss the unique needs of siblings in chapter 6.)

Consider the extended family. What are the grandparents'/aunts'/uncles'/cousins' opinions on gender ideology? Can extended family members be trusted to honor your authority and decisions, or are they likely to undermine you? Does the child have an especially good or especially bad relationship with any extended family members? Sometimes aunts and uncles seem much cooler and more sophisticated than parents do. Can you leverage a special relationship with an extended family member who may have an unusual amount of positive influence with your child?

Friends (Yours and Your Child's)

Which relationships are healthy and which are not? Do your friends agree with you about the harms the gender industry is perpetrating on children, or will they work behind your back to encourage your child in a false identity?

Are any of your child's friends trustworthy? Young people who are skeptical of gender ideology may be few and far between, since the gender industry has been very successful at getting kids indoctrinated. Which of your child's friends are feeding this delusion and which might help distract from it? Think of ways to support and encourage time spent with friends who are in the protagonist list. It's usually counterproductive to tell a child (especially a teenager) that he must or cannot spend time with certain people; announcing to your child that friends whom you placed in the antagonist list are forbidden might spur him or her toward these unhealthy influences rather than away from them. Instead, strategize ways to support the protagonists while discreetly moving your child away from the antagonists.

The School

Unfortunately, public schools today are either sold out to gender ideology or they're in the process of selling out. Private schools are falling as well, and recent events suggest that transgender-rights activists may now be targeting religious schools. In some places transgender-rights organizations have demanded that state departments of education report to them school districts which do not adopt the policies demanded by the gender industry.[124]

Are there specific teachers, counselors, administrators, or staff members that you know are either trustworthy or not trustworthy on this issue? Consider everyone who interacts with your child during the school day, including specialists such as speech and occupational therapists.

Do a bit of research on each of your child's teachers. Get teachers' names from your child or from the school's online database, or call the front office to ask for names. Peruse Facebook, Instagram, Twitter, LinkedIn, or other social media profiles. See what your child's teachers discuss, who they follow and like, and who their friends are in the school system and elsewhere. Follow or friend them anywhere you are able to do so. Google them to look for their names in news articles, letters to the editor, or for their group affiliations. It's usually not very difficult to determine if your child's teacher has an activist perspective toward gender ideology. If nothing else, visit the classroom; see what posters are on the wall and what books are on the shelves.

EXTRACURRICULAR ACTIVITIES

Where does your child spend free time? To what clubs does he or she belong, and who is also involved with those activities? Reach out to instructors, coaches, and team leaders. When you say, "My child recently announced a transgender identity," that person's initial response may tell you a great deal. "Oh, okay," might suggest discomfort, concern, or a lack of awareness about the gender industry. "Oh, that's wonderful!" tells you that you do not have an ally in that person.

If your child is in a national program with local chapters or groups, the program's website probably has policy information about things like discrimination and membership rules. See what the organization says about gender identity. If necessary, call the chapter leader or the state or national office. Ask specific questions such as, "What is your policy on transgender-identified children whose parents do not 'affirm'?"

Keep in mind, however, that activists are pushing hard to have children removed from homes where parents do not allow a child to pursue medicalization. Parents have lost custody of their own biological children over this issue.[125] If you sense antagonism from a group's leaders, it might be wise to cut ties with that group rather than risk being reported to a child protective services agency.

YOUR COMMUNITY

Do you live in a so-called "progressive" community that espouses "woke" programs and policies, or are your neighbors more conservative in their views? With whom does your child interact? Does he or she babysit or do yard work for any families? Who might be encountered at the playground or community center? Put these people into the protagonist and antagonist columns on your list.

Do you have a faith community or attend a house of worship? What does that faith teach about sex and personhood? How is the youth group handling kids who announce a transgender identity? Don't assume you know these answers, but ask specific questions, and be present as much as possible so you can see what's actually happening. One family discovered that the youth pastor had been calling their child by the trans name and preferred pronouns for two years, after the parents had specifically requested otherwise.

Upon finishing this exercise, you will probably have a very long list of antagonists and a fairly short list of protagonists. Recognizing this imbalance can threaten to overwhelm a parent with despair. But don't give up. Parents are getting their children back from the gender industry, even against titanic odds.

Children need all the adults in their lives to protect them, and to communicate and reflect truth to them. The adage "It takes a village to raise a child" has a lot to recommend it, except when the village is on fire, built in a war zone, or overpopulated with village idiots.

Today's global "village" may be suffering from all three maladies. Therefore, your challenge as a parent is to create for your child as safe and healthy a village as possible, while bricking up a robust wall to keep the flames, firefights, and fools on the outside.

Now that you've assessed the situation and built your team (as well as identified your opponents), you're ready to get to work.

Undertake a Campaign to Undo the Effects of Gender Brainwashing

Contact each person on your protagonist list individually. The closer each is to your child, the more information it's reasonable to provide. A grandparent who's known that child since infancy will certainly have more questions and concerns — and merit getting more personal information — than a karate instructor who only sees your child once a week.

Tell each protagonist what's going on:

> "Naomi recently announced to us that she believes she is nonbinary, which means she thinks she is neither a boy nor a girl. This doesn't make sense to us, and we think something else is going on. We wanted to ask if you'd be willing to support us toward encouraging Naomi to accept and love herself as a girl?"

Answer any questions you feel comfortable answering, but keep in mind that as much as you need team members to work alongside you, your child also deserves a certain amount of privacy. With the advent of the Internet, too many parents have opened up their children's entire lives to public scrutiny, posting on social media photos and stories that will haunt their children to the grave. These poor kids will enter adulthood with every foolish and embarrassing thing they ever did tattooed in perpetuity on the butt cheek of the Internet. Once it's on the World Wide Web, it never goes away.

Remember also that once you share information with another person, you have no control over what that person does with it. You would hate to tell your son's math teacher that he lacks nighttime bladder control, and then find out the teacher teased him about it in front of the class.

When you get agreement of support from a protagonist, be very clear about what you are asking that person to do:

✠ "Please use only Naomi's given name and the pronouns she/her. If she gets angry, you can tell her that we told you that's what we want, and you need to honor our authority."

✠ "We'd like you to tell us if she changes clothes after she comes to school."

✠ "Would you ask her out for breakfast once a month, and offer her a safe adult she can talk to who isn't one of her parents?"

✠ "If we want her to read an article or see a video about the harms of this ideology, could we send that to you to share with her since she admires you and respects your opinion?"

✠ "Could you possibly hire her to file papers or do some project at your office after school on Thursdays, so she isn't able to attend the GSA club?"

Get creative with your team. If your daughter has a standing Saturday-night babysitting gig with a family who is affirming her transition every chance they get, see if anyone on your team can come up with a Saturday-night job or activity for your daughter that's too sweet to pass up. If your son spends every free minute in online discussion groups that feed and reinforce the trans agenda, maybe one of his uncles can offer to take him on a week's surfing or skiing trip, to somewhere that happens not to have Wi-Fi.

Some parents who belong to faith traditions have written out and made copies of a special prayer or Scripture passage, so members of the team who also practice that faith tradition can all be praying or reciting that passage (and fasting, if that's a part of your faith tradition) for the child. This practice can bring great comfort and encouragement to parents during the potentially long journey from transgender identification to freedom.

After you've reached out to your list of protagonists, and set into place the things you'd like them to do, turn your attention to that long list of antagonists. Every unhealthy influence you can cut out of your child's life brings you a step closer to getting your child back.

Three ways exist to excise a person or group from your child's life. You can:

1. exert your authority to sever a relationship,

2. work behind the scenes to distract your child from a relationship, or

3. help your child make the decision to end a relationship.

EXERTING AUTHORITY TO SEVER A RELATIONSHIP

Although parental authority is under attack, it is still the law of the land in most places. If your child is a minor, you have the right to decide where your child will live, where your child will go to school, and who gets access to your child.

It may be necessary to pull your son or daughter from school. Anecdotal evidence points to positive outcomes for parents who withdraw their transgender-identified children from public school and homeschool them instead. This is an extreme decision to make if your children have always been in public school, but we know very well that public schools are promoting transgender ideology to the fullest extent of their power, and beyond. Lawsuits are almost certainly on the horizon, because public schools have flouted their responsibilities by not only skirting laws like the Federal Education Rights and Privacy Act and Title IX, but by trampling right over them.[126]

Some families have packed up and moved to get out of a school district or community that promoted gender theory to the extent that the parents felt they could not shield their child from it.

Families have taken away Internet access and/or electronic devices.

Parents often have the power of the purse strings. You needn't fund a summer camp that celebrates all things transgender. Don't renew the membership to the club or group that's affirming your child's transgender identity without your consent. Family members who undermine your authority by promoting transgender ideology behind your back don't get to spend time alone with your child. Period.

The drawback to the authoritative approach, however, is that kids do not like it one bit. Your child will push back, yell and scream, tell you you're a terrible parent, and do anything he or she can to fight you.

Your child may run away.

Your child may self-harm.

Your child may call a child protection agency on you.

You must be prepared for these possibilities. But you must also be honest with yourself about the chances of desistance if your child remains enmeshed with these negative influences. A year or two (or more) worth of hardship, struggling with an intractable and infuriated son or daughter, may prevent a lifetime of regret.

Distracting Your Child from a Relationship

When our kids were toddlers, and wanted more than anything to get Grandma's antique vase off the mantel or were fixated on the chocolate cake on the counter, redirecting their attention by removing the temptation or by offering something more interesting often proved a more successful technique than trying to enforce, "I said no!"

Likewise, an easier and less domineering strategy when they're tweens or teenagers may be working behind the scenes to remove unhealthy relationships wherever possible.

If your son has friends that are on your antagonist list, let him know that they are welcome to come to your house, but you're not comfortable with him going to theirs. (If the friends know you're not affirming the transgender identification, they may not want to visit you.) If your daughter joined the GSA club that meets during lunch on Fridays, see if the teacher who's on your protagonist list can get your daughter to lead a book club for younger students at the same time or invite her to spend a few weeks painting sets for the school play. If one of your kids mows lawns for neighbors who invite him in for cookies, lemonade, and gender affirmation after he finishes his work, it may be worth "breaking" your lawnmower and hiring a yard service for yourself for the summer.

If you can find a way to make the undesirable relationship more difficult for your child to sustain, without actually throwing down a command or ultimatum, your child will have less ammunition for calling you a hateful, bigoted dictator.

Utilize your team for distancing and distracting your child from unhealthy relationships and situations. Brainstorm with members of your team when you have a difficult situation you're not sure how to handle.

LEADING YOUR CHILD TO DECIDE
TO END A RELATIONSHIP

By far, the best path is when the child decides to leave unhealthy relationships or situations. If you are able to gently guide your child to a good decision by asking leading questions, you will accomplish two very important things: first, the destructive relationship will be ended with no sense of unfairness or parental overreach from your child; second, you will have strengthened your relationship with your child by providing him or her a sense of autonomy and personal choice.

Remember that beyond your immediate goal of getting your child to accept his or her birth sex as reality, your overarching goal as a parent should be to turn out a healthy adult who can make responsible decisions and lead a productive and positive life. That doesn't happen overnight but emerges through an ongoing relationship as you back off exerting control over your growing child and start letting him or her take responsibility for decisions. This is part of the finesse we talked about in chapter 1: each child is different, each parent is different, and each family is different, so figuring out how to negotiate these decisions is never simple.

Recently our daughter was invited by an adult in our community — I'll call her Mrs. O. — to play Dungeons & Dragons, the game at the center of the *Stranger Things* TV show. The group was composed of both teens and adults.

A few things bothered me about the situation. First, my daughter's friend gave my daughter's contact information to Mrs. O. without permission. Second, Mrs. O. emailed my daughter without ever contacting me or my husband. Third, it seemed strange to me both that teenagers would want to play "D & D" with their parents, and that an adult seemed to be orchestrating the games.

"I don't really know anything about D & D," my daughter admitted. "But would I be allowed to go?"

A number of recent issues with my daughter had required her father and me to make authoritative decisions that she didn't like, so I was surprised and pleased that she asked permission so respectfully. I decided to try to walk her toward rejecting this invitation herself.

"Before we decide whether you should go or not," I began, "there are a couple of things that bother me, and I'd like to find out what you think." I asked if she had given her friend permission to share her email address with Mrs. O.

"No, I didn't," she said. "That kind of bothers me too."

"Yeah. That's bad form. You should always get permission before sharing someone's contact information."

We'd agreed on the first point. That was huge. So, I went on to discuss what I considered the bigger deal.

"I'm more troubled by the fact that Mrs. O. emailed you without contacting me."

When my kids got email accounts, we let them know that we would have access to their accounts until they turned eighteen. Everything that comes into my kids' inboxes gets copied to mine, and they're aware of that. So I saw Mrs. O.'s email to my daughter.

No adult should communicate with a child without the knowledge of that child's parents. Why? Because nefarious adults exist who would do harm to children. I have no idea who the predatory people are, but my radar for identifying them is much savvier than my kids' radars.

An adult who has good intentions toward a child has no reason to fear the child's parents being involved in the relationship. An adult with bad intentions has every reason to fear the parents' involvement. Circumventing a child's parents indicates either bad intentions or a profound lack of courtesy, common sense, or respect.

If I need to communicate with one of my kids' friends for any reason, I either contact the child's parents or I ask my child to communicate with the friend on my behalf. An adult who does not afford me the same respect when it comes to my children does not get access to my children.

I consulted a trusted friend about the situation to confirm I wasn't just being paranoid. She responded:

> Yeah, I don't know what the woman's motive is. I would love to chill out and trust that it was a harmless invite to join a harmless group of gamers. Sadly, I've seen and heard far too much. Harmless people seem to be the exception now rather than the rule. It used to be unthinkable to override another parent and cover for another's kid. I even saw it with my own son. His friends' parents would lie for the kids. I was lied to by other mothers, people I truly considered friends. It was quite disheartening to say the least. They presented as caring parents but behind the scenes were allowing and even being a part of pretty promiscuous behavior. It wasn't uncommon for some to purchase alcohol so kids would come hang out with their kid (they wanted their child to be popular). It's all fine and dandy till several kids landed in the ER with alcohol poisoning. The mom lost custody of her own kids because she was passed out drunk in her closet while kids were going wild in her house.

My daughter and I talked through Mrs. O.'s behavior.

"Doesn't it seem kind of weird," I asked, "for teenagers to be playing D & D with their parents? Would you want your dad and me to play board games with you and your friends?"

Her eyes grew wide. "No. Never."

"That's what I thought. Why do you think Mrs. O. is organizing these games with both kids and adults?"

"I don't know. That does seem kind of weird."

"Yeah."

We'd agreed on the second point. My daughter and I didn't need to understand Mrs. O.'s actual intentions, we only needed to agree that her behavior was suspect.

"Why don't you take some time to think about whether you really want to go or not. If you decide you want to play with them, then your dad and I can talk about it some more," I suggested.

The next day she told me she wasn't interested in the invitation.

I couldn't have been more pleased or proud.

Groomers

The Dungeons & Dragons story leads, unfortunately, to the issue of groomers.

In chapter 1 we looked at how transgender ideology fits neatly into what we know about how cults operate. Similarly, the gender industry's tactics perfectly parallel how child predators groom their targets for exploitation.[127]

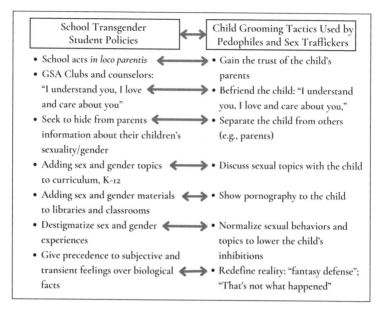

School Transgender Student Policies	Child Grooming Tactics Used by Pedophiles and Sex Traffickers
• School acts *in loco parentis*	• Gain the trust of the child's parents
• GSA Clubs and counselors: "I understand you, I love and care about you"	• Befriend the child: "I understand you, I love and care about you,"
• Seek to hide from parents information about their children's sexuality/gender	• Separate the child from others (e.g., parents)
• Adding sex and gender topics to curriculum, K-12	• Discuss sexual topics with the child
• Adding sex and gender materials to libraries and classrooms	• Show pornography to the child
• Destigmatize sex and gender experiences	• Normalize sexual behaviors and topics to lower the child's inhibitions
• Give precedence to subjective and transient feelings over biological facts	• Redefine reality: "fantasy defense"; "That's not what happened"

Social media influencers are boldly doing the very thing that should terrify, infuriate, and engage parents: these transgender-identified "mentors" — who are primarily adult men pretending to be women — invite children to call them, email them, and in some cases even come live with them. Munroe Bergdorf — the woman-*née*-man whom a major cosmetics company hired as their first transgender spokesperson and then fired days later after he tweeted out a racist rant — encourages young, transgender-identified kids to contact him: "To any trans kids out there who want or need support. Please @ me.... Drop me a message on insta [sic]."[128]

Parents' predator radars should scream like sirens when an adult man suggests that children contact him on the side.

One of the most powerful predictors of academic success is parental involvement, and the most significant force for stability in a society is the intact nuclear family.[129] No adults are more influential in a child's life than his or her parents. No other relationship — save potentially with a spouse — will have as long a history, as deep a present, and as far-reaching a future in that child's life. The parent-child relationship has been respected and honored throughout human history and across cultures.

Until now.

When something or someone seeks to sever or come between the relationship between a parent and child, except in cases of extreme parental neglect or abuse, that separation is almost always enacted for nefarious reasons, often resulting in victimization of the child.[130] Isolating a child from parents or guardians is one of the calculated steps that pedophiles and predators take in order to groom a child for sexual abuse.[131]

One such tactic is revealed in the following excerpt from the *New Yorker*. Malcolm Gladwell relates psychologist Carla van Dam's story about her work with former teacher and convicted pedophile Jeffrey Clay.

> Clay ... first put himself in a place with easy access to children — an elementary school. Then he worked his way through his class. He began by simply asking boys if they wanted to stay after school. "Those who could not do so without parental permission were screened out," van Dam writes. Children with vigilant parents are too risky.[132]

Public schools are falling like dominoes to transgender activists' demands, one of which is that the school step in between children and their parents, both with respect to what is taught and modeled regarding gender ideology, and how children identify themselves with respect to their sexuality and gender identity. Unless the school and the child are confident that parents will fully capitulate to and applaud an alternate sex identity, the school and child are instructed — commanded, in fact — to keep the parents in the dark and out of the picture.[133]

Parents should not tolerate anyone's subversion of their authority over their own children. If your child's school has a policy, history, or evidence of hiding anything from parents, that school is no longer a trustworthy place to send children. When adults reach out to your child behind your back, those adults are not trustworthy people to allow in your child's life.

Every adult who hides from you his or her interactions with your child is treacherous, dangerous, and toxic to your child and your family. Even child protection agencies knock on your front door if they suspect abuse in your home. The only people who sneak around with children are predators, even if it's your sweet Aunt Millicent who just can't see what's wrong with letting Elijah call himself Ellie.

The stakes are far too high for our children to be trusted to anyone who doesn't respect our authority as parents.

Summary: A Plan for Deprogramming Transgender-Identified Children

Throughout this difficult journey, we always want to keep in mind our goals and strategies for drawing our kids out of the gender cult:

1. We focus always on the end goal: for the child to accept reality and his or her body and birth sex.

2. We develop a team of protagonists to help us work toward our goal.

3. We strive to cut off from relationship with our child as many antagonists as possible.

4. We work to improve our entire relationship with our child, and to minimize how much of the child's life revolves around gender ideology.

5. Our team prepares for and anticipates opportunities to have strategic conversations with the child, whereby we can plant questions and seeds of doubt about the gender industry's doctrine.

When this nightmare descends on a family, it's natural that the parents' first inclination is to look for the thing that will make it stop right now: What is the right word, the right argument, the right therapist, the right response that will end this horror immediately?

Unfortunately, it's rarely that easy to extract someone from a cult. The gender cult is pernicious, ubiquitous, and zealous to keep its victims in its clutches. Parents may be all that stand between their child and the gender industry. Therefore, parents must exercise patience, tenacity, finesse, and most of all unconditional, tough, and determined love.

CHAPTER 5

Unfailing Love

*"Being deeply loved by someone gives you strength,
while loving someone deeply gives you courage."*

— Attributed to Lao Tzu

THE CONCEPT OF LOVE has undergone tremendous abuse in modern parlance: it's been redefined as sex, lust, passion, obsession, infatuation, stalking, mistreatment, coercion, permissiveness, tolerance, indulgence, codependence, and a host of various other things that actually don't relate much to its real meaning. The gender industry claims that *love* means giving someone anything and everything he or she wants, and never saying anything he or she doesn't want to hear.

None of these ideas defines what it means to love someone.

When my grandmother began showing signs of dementia and started writing checks to anyone who came to her door and claimed she owed him money, her kids took away her checkbook and seized control of her finances to protect her from financial ruin. She was furious with them. They did it anyway. That was love.

When her college boyfriend broke up with her, Tania cried on her friend Mary's shoulder. "Of course he left me for that other girl. She's prettier than I am, and she's more popular and cooler, and she dresses better than I do." Mary asked Tania, "Is that really what's

113

important to you, and what you want a man to want you for? That you're the prettiest and the coolest and have the best clothes? I thought you were a little deeper than that." Tania's pride was stung, but she knew Mary was right. That was love.

A man turns down the attractive coworker who went beyond her usual flirtatiousness and invited him out for drinks after work, despite how much he really wants to go out with her. He leaves the office early to keep an appointment with his estranged wife for marriage therapy, honoring a commitment he made at his wedding all those years ago: "Till death do us part." That's love.

Love is keeping my promises. Love is putting someone else's good above my own. Love is a choice I make and a day-after-day commitment to look after someone else's best interests, even when it costs me dearly.

And love is apologizing and making amends when I fall short.

Walking children through the journey out of the gender cult requires us to love in ways that we may not have experienced or expressed before.

Unconditional Love

Early in chapter 2 we read the very first thing parents must do when a child announces a transgender identity: "Assure your child that you love him or her, no matter what."

You continue to love your child:

- ✤ whether he behaves the way you want, or not.
- ✤ whether she selects clothes and a hairstyle you prefer, or not.
- ✤ no matter what he says to or about you.

- if she self-harms with drugs or razor blades or dieting or surgeries.
- when he hurts you or hurts other people you love.
- even if she says, "I hate you," and demonstrates it with every word and every choice.

You won't always feel loving toward your child. There may be times when you're so worn down from the fight, you think that maybe it would be easier to just give in and let the child take the hormones and have the surgeries. You might secretly, just for a moment, wish your child would make good on the threat to run away, so the rest of the family could get on with their lives and stop walking on eggshells while praying things will get better. It may take every bit of self-control you've got not to say, "I don't care! Go ahead! Destroy your health and your future, if that's what you want so badly. I can't deal with you anymore!"

Unconditional love means choosing not to do those things, no matter how much you want to. And it means apologizing and asking forgiveness if you do them.

Every child desperately aches for unconditional love from his or her parents. And every child pushes back against that love, especially during the teenage years. This happens partly as a function of growing up and preparing to leave the nest. Children need to separate from their parents and establish their own identity apart from what they've inherited from the family. This feature of adolescence is what makes this ideology so insidious — the gender industry preys upon kids right where they live.

But even when children are behaving like cretinous little ingrates, they still need their parents to love them. They still want to know that we are steadfast in our commitment to them. They need parents whose love for them will never switch off or dry up.

Every one of us longs for that kind of love. We can't force anyone to give it to us, but we can commit to giving it to others. And we can give it whether we *feel* it or not, because it's a choice we make, not an emotion we follow.

Children who have been recruited by the gender cult need unconditional love desperately. In Appendix A you'll find messages from desisters and detransitioners about what they needed from their parents during this difficult journey. Their words whisper of a deep yearning for their parents' love.

However, unconditional love is not a coward, nor is it a doormat that never says no.

Tough Love

The gender industry claims that "Kids know who they are," even from infancy, and that we should "Let children lead." But when one of my kids was in preschool, she insisted for months that she was Cleopatra, and if I'd let my toddlers lead, they'd have washed down their chocolate bars and candy canes with bottles of pancake syrup at every single meal, every single day.

Tough love makes good decisions that aren't popular, and then enforces them with appropriate consequences.

THE CHILDREN ARE NOT IN CHARGE

Mom and Dad are the bosses. What they say, goes. A loving family is not a democracy; it is a benevolent dictatorship with a long view toward the independent sovereignty of the governed.

But isn't that unfair?

No, it is not unfair, because the adults have the experience, the wisdom (hopefully), and the responsibility for the safety and welfare of their home and their family.

The snaggle-toothed ankle-biter who licks the bottom of his own shoe does not get to decide whether or not he will wear his coat outside, how long he will stay at the grocery store, or what time he will go to bed at night.

The thirteen-year-old doesn't set his own curfew, send dinner back to the kitchen and order an upgraded meal, or decide that his homework is optional.

The high schooler doesn't get to take the family car without permission, skip school because he stayed up too late bingeing movies the night before, or smoke cigarettes in the garage.

Children follow the rules of the house set by Mom and Dad, because if they don't, they go to Kid Hell.

Mom and Dad Are the Gatekeepers and the Keymasters of Kid Hell

Kid Hell is the place your child least wishes to be. It is the environment or situation he will do anything to avoid.

It's the playpen when she won't stop pulling the cat's tail.

It's losing his blankie or his favorite plush snuggle bear for the night when he consistently refuses to get in bed and stay there.

It's alone in the bedroom when he won't speak respectfully to his parents, siblings, or friends.

It's the front of the grocery cart, facing Mom, legs through the square holes. If the eight-year-old throws a tantrum in the candy aisle, her round little butt goes in the cart's baby seat, even if it gives Mom a herniated disc to put her there.

It's holding Mom's hand to cross the street, when the ten-year-old can't or won't remember to look both ways first.

It's Dad attending every single class, all day long, with the middle-schooler who bullies other kids, or uses inappropriate language in school, or claims the teachers *never* assign homework.

It's taking away the car keys and garnishing the high school student's part-time-job wages until he covers the repairs on the car that he banged up doing donuts in the school parking lot.

It's evicting the twenty-three-year-old who sits on the couch playing video games all day and night, refusing to contribute to the household via rent or work.

WE ARE NOT OUR KIDS' FRIENDS

If we do our job well, we will be our children's friends someday, when they become independent and responsible adults. Until then, we are advocates, mentors, tutors, cheerleaders, confidantes, counselors, managers, taskmasters, spiritual guides, parole officers, and trainers. But we are not their friends.

When we take on the role of friend, we abdicate all other positions. And if we don't fill those positions, our children will find other people who will: those roles will likely be offered to peers, social media influencers, and/or predatory glitter-moms.

TOUGH LOVE SAYS WHAT IT MEANS
AND MEANS WHAT IT SAYS

Children must believe that their parents' words have meaning and are trustworthy.

If the house rule says that dessert only follows a clean dinner plate, then the kid with an uneaten serving of peas gets no ice cream.

If Dad says he will take away the PlayStation if his son misbehaves, and then his son misbehaves, Dad must take away the PlayStation.

If parents say there will be no trip to the waterpark until all the homework is finished, the truant homework-er will not see the wave pool till the last science problem is finished correctly and legibly.

Likewise, if Mom and Dad say they'll take the kids to the opening night of the latest superhero movie, or that they'll go out for burgers tonight, or that they'll sign the kids up for space camp, Mom and Dad need to make good on those offers. When children know that parents follow through on their words — both threats and promises — they feel *safe*, even if they complain endlessly about how unfair we are.

Tough Love Is Hard Work

Children begin life as beautiful, kissable little creatures who frequently behave like deranged little savages. They will not turn out to be responsible, self-regulating, successful adults just because we want them to, just like nobody will hand me a bag of money because I sit on a bench in front of the bank and hope for the best.

Kids are clever, selfish, willful, manipulative, obstinate, petulant, impulsive, and wildly creative human beings. And sometimes they go wildly off the rails. They desperately need parents who love them enough to be tough. We must lower our heads, steel our nerves, and meet the challenge.

If parenting were easy, a child could do it.

Determined Love

It bears repeating that working with a child who has been recruited by the gender industry is a long and arduous process. You are trying to create a protective village around your child to reawaken his or her mind and lead the child into freedom; the gender industry has already surrounded your child with a village that manipulates your child's emotions and celebrates self-harm. You're trying to erect a wall to keep lies and destructive influences away from your child; the gender industry has already constructed a wall around him or her to keep truth and protective influences out. You are building up and tearing down at the same time. This is very hard work. You must commit from the outset to stay the course and never give up.

Dual Identities

Remember that people who have been indoctrinated into cults have been manipulated emotionally into allowing the cult identity to overtake their true identities. This is why you no longer recognize your child, and why he or she seems to have turned into an entirely different person. Remaking your child into fodder for the gender industry's medicalization machine is precisely the cult's goal, because transgender medicine and politics are a billion-dollar industry.[134]

As you work the strategy to pull your child out of the gender cult, you are actually dealing with two different people: your child's true identity and the cult identity. Pulling your child out of the cult really means helping the child rediscover and love his or her true self so that the false and destructive cult self can be discarded.

You're probably dealing with your child's true identity when

- ✛ he or she remembers events accurately.
- ✛ he or she "sounds" like him- or herself: using language, inflections, and subjects that you recognize as part of the child's real personality or interests.
- ✛ he or she is relaxed, noncombative, and seems relatively at peace.

You're likely dealing with the cult identity when

- ✛ memories of events are distorted or fabricated.
- ✛ the child's words sound scripted or programmed, filled with sloganeering and language that's particular to the cult.

✠ he or she is tense, angry, combative, and seems to be looking for a fight or a reason to leave.

Parents of transgender-identified children often express bewilderment
and frustration because one day (or minute) their child seems fairly
pleasant and easy to get along with, then the next day (or minute) the
child morphs into a cyclone of volatility and aggression. This happens
because two identities are at war inside the child. The true identity
wants freedom; it wants to express itself and live. But the cult identity
is powerful, intimidating, and determined.

You may have heard the Native American legend about two men
discussing the internal struggle between good and evil. The elder
said, "It is like two dogs fighting inside you to the death." The
younger man asked the elder, "Which dog will win?" The elder re-
plied, "Whichever dog you feed."

Feed your child's true identity. Nurture your relationship. Encourage and affirm the child in all the positive things about his or her
real self. Spend quality time together, to bring the child's mind and
heart back into identification and alignment with him- or herself and
with your family.

Starve the cult identity. Cut it off from its food sources. Challenge its assumptions and assertions. Do not give in to its
unacceptable demands. Give it no quarter.

Signs of Desistance and Boomeranging

Parents whose kids have successfully left the gender cult describe a
strange phenomenon that seems to be common among desisters and
detransitioners.

The parents will begin to have successful interactions, during
which the child may grow silent rather than continue to argue, or
may even agree that the parent has made a good point.

Such moments are signs that the cult identity is weakening and the true self is emerging and reengaging the child's mind.

Other positive signs include

✢ the child making a choice (of clothing, hairstyle, activity) that is representative of his or her "old" style or personality, or of something stereotypical of his or her birth sex.

✢ the child making light of something about gender ideology. One parent reported that her daughter offered to fetch something off a high shelf that Mom couldn't reach. The mother said, "But you're not taller than I am," to which the child responded, "But I identify as a tall person," and then laughed. The child desisted a few months later.

✢ the child criticizing something about gender ideology or the gender community.

✢ the child reengaging an interest that was dropped upon entering the cult, such as picking up an abandoned musical instrument or going back to a previous fixation (in the case of someone on the autism spectrum) that ended abruptly upon identifying as transgender.

✢ the child dropping an interest or activity that began when he or she identified with the cult. One prodigious artist started creating detailed and extraordinary paintings that represented very dark and macabre subjects. This continued throughout the cult identification. Not long before the child desisted, the parents saw the artwork begin to move away from such occultic and nightmarish themes.

✢ the child reconnecting with a relationship that was abandoned upon entering the cult, such as contacting a friend or relative who didn't affirm the cult identity.

✛ parents and the team having more (and more frequent) interactions with the child's true identity, and fewer with the cult identity.

The fascinating and frustrating experience that parents report, however, is that very often, after the parent observes one of these encouraging signs, the child boomerangs hard, back into the cult identity:

✛ The child doubles down on some belief or thought-stopping slogan around gender ideology.

✛ He or she reverts fanatically to presenting as transgender. One girl painted her nails pink, causing her mother to silently shout, "Hallelujah!"; the very next day the girl wrote "He" and "Him" on every one of her pink fingernails with a Sharpie.

✛ The child's cult identity attacks the parent with whom the true identity had a positive interaction, perhaps out of the blue, accusing the parent of being transphobic, hateful, and the like.

At the time of this writing, there seems to be no research or data on this phenomenon, which I call *boomeranging*, but anecdotal evidence is emerging regularly.

This back-and-forth does make sense, when viewed through the lens of competing identities: the child has put on the cult identity because the gender industry successfully exploited some vulnerability in the child; the child feels safety and protection within the cult community, and is likely terrified (with good reason, considering how the cult treats those who leave) at the idea of exiting the cult. The cult has indoctrinated the child with the belief that those outside the cult are dangerous, toxic, and hostile. As the child begins to discover that this is not true, his or her loyalties are challenged, as though the cult is yanking on one of the child's arms and the family is holding firmly to the other.

Self-Love

Parents must care well for themselves as they're struggling on this journey with a transgender-identified child. You are pouring unconditional, tough, and determined love into your child, devoting time and attention to seize every opportunity to interact with your child in ways that will draw him or her back into the family and into reality, while at the same time battling all the forces of the culture that are trying to snare and keep hold of your child.

This may be the hardest work you ever do as a parent.

You can't pour anything out of an empty vessel, so you need to make sure that your needs are also being cared for throughout this demanding season in your family's life.

✠ Tap into your protagonists when you need support for yourself. Schedule a weekly coffee date or a monthly golf game with your best friend. Find one or two people who are willing to be available to you by phone or text when you wake up crying or terrified or angry in the middle of the night.

✠ Do things that give you life. If working out restores your sense of peace and balance, make sure you get to the gym regularly, or that you have exercise equipment at home that you use on a regular schedule. If painting, knitting, or sculpting feed your soul, make space for enjoying those during your week. If you need to climb a big rock or scale a fifteen-foot wall to get the angst out of your muscles and mind, spend the time and money it takes to give that to yourself.

✣ Journaling — unless you absolutely loathe writing — can be a great practice during difficult periods. Write down the hard things and the moments of light. You'll be able to see trends emerge over the months, and when you feel disheartened you can go back and remember those instances when you saw your child's true identity resurface.

✣ If you have a faith community, ask someone to establish a prayer or meditation circle for you and your family. Tell them what needs you have as those issues arise, so they can lift those up for you.

There's one more important thing I want to recommend that you do for yourself. It's going to seem counterintuitive, and perhaps even cruel. It's one of the last things a parent ever wants to consider, and it's exactly the outcome that this book is trying to help you avoid. But if you can come to terms with it, and release the powerful desire to exert control over it, you may come to a mysterious sense of peace.

Accept that you may lose your child.

From the moment our children are conceived, we have not one guarantee or promise that we will have them for another day. Pregnancies miscarry. Babies are stillborn. Children get cancer. Teenagers die in accidents and by their own hands. None of us have any assurance that our own hearts will beat even one more time.

While you fight with everything you have to save your child from this heinous cult, let yourself rest in the knowledge that you do not have control over the situation, the child, or the outcome. You strive to parent and to love that child to the very best of your ability, but ultimately the future is out of your hands. All of us — including our children — get to choose what we will do with our lives. Others cannot impose their wills upon us.

It isn't your fault that your child got sucked into this cult, and you don't have the power to force him or her out of it.

A strange and bittersweet freedom can come to us when we acquiesce to that truth.

As we close our discussion on love, it may be helpful to reflect on the words of the meditation used by so many who struggle through painful seasons:

> *God, grant me the serenity*
> *to accept the things I cannot change,*
> *courage to change the things I can,*
> *and the wisdom to know the difference.*

CHAPTER 6
The Rest of the Family

"Our daughter became physical and violent....
She controlled and threatened her sisters before
she seemed to have an identity fixation."

— Parent whose daughter had mental health issues;
therapists would not address anything but gender

Don't let everything in your family become all about the transgender issue. One parent told a transgender-identified child who sought to make everything in the home about gender, "I get that you're struggling with this, and we want to help. But in the meantime, the rest of us have our own lives to lead and we're going to do that." Don't give gender ideology any more power than it already has.

Caring for Your Marriage

Any issues related to a child's physical or psychological health can put a significant strain on the parents' marriage. When it comes to gender ideology, the parents' relationship will suffer greater impact if they do not agree on the treatment path that's best for the child. Parents who are divorced and/or living apart have even more strikes against them with respect to working together, even if they are amicable and agree on not affirming the transgender identity. If stepparents are involved in the picture as well, that can mean more protagonist-adults in the safe village, or it can mean more antagonist-adults working against you as you try to cut off unhealthy influences.

The topic of relationships around divorce and remarriage is far too complex to delve into here. If you are in a strained marriage, or negotiating these issues with ex-spouses and stepparents, please find a good family therapist who can help you work through the problems facing you. Your child is in crisis and needs to have access to the healthiest, strongest adult relationships possible.

If your family situation is fairly simple, you still may find that dealing with your transgender-identified child sparks friction between you and your spouse.

- Keep lines of communication open. Use the relationship skills discussed in chapter 3 to have productive and positive discussions with your spouse, not only about the gender issue but about everything you face as a family.
- When you disagree, try to credit your spouse with good intentions. Everyone has reasons for what they believe, what they want, and what they do; try to understand where your spouse is coming from before demanding that your spouse consider your perspective.
- Go on weekly dates, if possible. You married this person because you enjoyed his or her company and liked spending time together. Regularly spending time alone with your spouse can help you remember what you like about each other and put you back into *we're-on-the-same-team* mode.
- Show your spouse appreciation. Thank him or her for everything you can. A wise person once said, "Keep both eyes open before marriage, and one eye closed after." Try to

focus on the positive more than the negative, unless you are dealing with abuse.

☦ If you or your children are experiencing abuse from your spouse, or if your relationship has become strained past the point that you have any hope for improvement, seek professional help right away.

The Special Needs of Siblings

When a child announces a transgender identity, the whole family is profoundly affected. It's easy and understandable for parents to spend significant time and energy coping with the child who is going through the identity crisis, but it's important to recognize that the other children in the family are suffering as well.

Your other kids need special, individual support from their parents to navigate this unprecedented and painful experience. Children whose brother or sister claims to be other than his or her birth sex may find themselves confused, frightened, hurt, and in need of both guidance and authoritative backup regarding interactions with their sibling.

WHAT SIBLINGS MAY EXPERIENCE

Depending on the age of your children and the birth order around the child who is claiming a transgender identity, emotional reactions to and the stress of interactions with their brother or sister may vary widely. Younger children may feel confused and frightened, while older or adult children's responses may run the gamut between anger and applause, and between severing the relationship with the sibling to severing the relationship with you, if you do not capitulate to your child's newly announced identity change.

Siblings younger than the transgender-identified child may feel bewildered by the sudden loss of the older sibling as the familiar and perhaps admired brother or sister, and they may experience significant bullying from the transgender-identified sibling to participate in the sibling's new identity, "or else." Brothers and sisters who are older than the transgender-identified child may respond with derision or eye-rolling, and may also land anywhere on the spectrum between embarrassment about and pride in their sibling.

Cognitive Dissonance

Children whose sibling claims to be transgender will experience some level of cognitive dissonance, which is the mental discomfort one experiences when two worldviews or perceptions of reality conflict with each other.

It is neither normal nor possible for a person to change sex. Children who understand that boys have a penis and girls have a vagina — the most basic of physiological categorizations, grasped by the age of three or four years — will have their worldview upended by their sibling's announcement that she or he is no longer she or he.

The gender industry has spent an enormous amount of time, effort, and money to convince society that transgenderism is praiseworthy, pride-worthy, and normal, but no matter how many times one repeats a lie, the lie becomes no truer. Believing a lie only dislodges one from reality and requires one to accommodate ever more erroneous beliefs in order to support that lie, such as:

⤚ **"Males have no physiological advantages over females in sports."**
(*Yes, they do.*)

⤚ **"Girls who don't want boys in their bathrooms are bigots and transphobes."**
(*No, they're not.*)

✠ **"Some women have penises and some men have vaginas."**
(No, they don't.)

All children need their parents to be anchors to truth and reality; siblings of transgender-identified children (and the transgender-identified children themselves) need this firm foundation from their parents in spades. Reiterate to your children what you believe to be true:

> "I realize that your brother John thinks he's a girl. He is confused right now and has been misled about what's real and true. People cannot change sex, and no person was ever born in the wrong body. Your body is you, and there's no research or data to support the idea that our minds can be a different 'gender' from our bodies. We are going to love John and support him toward accepting this truth for himself, but we are not going to agree with something that simply isn't true."

Fear, Hurt, and Blame

Cognitive dissonance, if unresolved, can lead to fear, both about the specific situation and about life in general. The child may worry about his sibling's health and well-being, as well as wonder what else in the world might not be as he believed it to be. As Colin Wright so aptly explained, "I'm frequently asked why I focus so much on the nature of biological sex. It's because in my view this may be reality's last stand. If this undeniable fact can be denied *en masse,* then we become hostages to chaos. We simply cannot afford to lose our collective tether to reality."[135]

Although your child may not be able to articulate or even be fully conscious of this thought process, he recognizes deep down that if the basis of our most intimate sense of identity is not fixed, then nothing else in life is fixed either. There are no boundaries, no truths, no solid foundations on which to stand. This is a terrifying thought for anyone, but especially for a child.

Additionally, when a person announces a transgender identity, the effect on family and friends is similar to experiencing the death of a loved one. Men and women are not interchangeable one for the other; they are entirely different beings.

If a woman announced that she is no longer Louise Archer but is now Joan of Arc, we would rightly recognize that she is rejecting herself and attempting to appropriate someone else's existence. This is no less true of transgender claims: the transgender-identified person is trying to kill who he or she has been, as evidenced by terms like "deadname" in reference to the now-rejected name that was given to a child by parents.

A sibling may also feel rejected by the transgender-identified child, and perhaps even more so if they are the same biological sex. It's possible the child may wonder if he or she is somehow to blame for the situation. Ruminating on past conflicts and words hurled in the heat of anger may lead the child to conclude that his or her anger, mistakes, or personality caused the sibling to want to change sex. Further, if parents focus solely on dealing with the transgender-identified child, the other children in the family may feel less important, less loved, or simply neglected by comparison.

Always validate a child's feelings, but always correct flawed thinking:

> "Yes, this is a very hurtful situation. John is rejecting himself right now, and he's also rejecting our family to a certain degree. But this is not your fault, nor is it Mom's or my fault. We're not a perfect family, but we love each other and we're doing our best. We love

John very much, and we love you just as much. That will never change."

Bullying

The transgender-identified child will likely try to bully everyone into submitting to preferred names, pronouns, and beliefs about identity and personhood. A younger child in the household is especially at risk of being manipulated and coerced into behaving according to the transgender-identified child's wishes:

✠ "I'll turn off my music so you can go to sleep after you name five different genders."

✠ "Watch this YouTube video about misgendering, or I'll tell everyone at school about how you suck your thumb while you sleep."

✠ "I'm not responding to my "deadname" anymore. If you call me that I'll not only ignore you, I'll hit you."

✠ "If you don't use the pronouns I want, I'll kill myself. When I die it will be your fault."

Much of this intimidation is likely to happen behind Mom's and Dad's backs, so you'll need to keep open ears, open eyes, and open lines of communication with all of your kids. Set boundaries, and communicate them clearly:

✠ "You are not to discuss sexuality or gender ideology with your younger siblings."

✠ "There will be no use of the Internet other than for schoolwork."

✠ "In this house you will be called by the name we gave you and by the appropriate pronouns."

Children try to bully their parents, too. One young lady told her parents in a note left on their bed, "I am no longer responding to the name 'Jessica' or to the pronouns 'she/her.' If you use them, I will simply ignore you." Her parents left a response on her bed: "Your legal name, given to you legally by your parents, is Jessica, and the grammatically correct pronouns for girls are she/her. If you fail to respond when these are used to address you, there will be consequences." That was the end of the discussion. (Jessica eventually accepted herself as female and abandoned the transgender narrative.)

Supporting Siblings

Remember how the gender cult works: Vulnerable people are drawn in with promises of nirvana and a community of supportive people who will escort them to that nirvana. They are brainwashed with lies, taught how to use a brand-new lexicon in order to be part of the group, and severed from those who love them the most. As painful as this experience is for you, it can be equally traumatic for your other kids.

Talk to your children about what's going on as early as possible and as often as they wish. Soon after the transgender-identified child's announcement, sit down with your other kids — individually, if you can — and help them understand and process it. Be as factual as possible, use age-appropriate language, and try to keep your own emotions in check (whether you're angry, sad, bewildered, or all three), so your child doesn't feel like he or she needs to withhold heavy feelings or questions from you in order to protect your emotional state. The child needs you to be strong, straightforward, and loving: "John gave me some troubling information this week about who he thinks he really is. I wanted to talk to you about it to find out if you have any questions or concerns, or if there's anything you want to ask about."

Dealing with a child who identifies as transgender can be a long journey. As you walk together through this as a family, occasionally get each of your children alone for some special time together, and ask a few open-ended questions:

- ☩ "How are you feeling about John (or about our family) right now?"
- ☩ "Is there anything that worries or confuses you?"
- ☩ "Is there anything I can help you with? Is there anything you need me to do?"

If your child seems to be having an especially hard time with this (or with anything), consider finding a trustworthy therapist to help you. Be very cautious that you find a counselor whose position on the transgender narrative matches yours. This is becoming increasingly difficult to do as transgender activists have been successful in enacting laws preventing therapists from doing anything except affirm a child's sex transition. (We'll discuss how to find a trustworthy therapist later in this chapter.)

And finally, work toward the improved health of your entire family. Strengthen all relationships as much as you can: eat meals together, do activities together, talk about the little things and the big things, and communicate to everyone in your family that you are a team and that you love each other. If you end every conversation and interaction with a hug (provided the child will accept one) and the words "I love you," you'll be on the right track.

Extended Family Issues

In chapter 4 we touched upon sorting extended family members (grandparents, aunts, uncles, etc.) into the lists of protagonists and antagonists. You may not know which category one of your relatives falls into until after you or your child has shared the child's announcement. It's generally best to tell the child that informing extended family members is his or her job, rather than making life easy for the kid by doing it yourself. Informing others of this situation can be emotionally draining work, so don't saddle yourself with it if you don't have to.

When someone comes out as transgender, reactions tend to fall into one of two categories:

> 1. "That's amazing! Congratulations! That's so awesome! We support you 100 percent!"

or

> 2. "Oh. Okay. I'm not sure I understand. What?"

People who react to the news like they just won a pony and a million dollars are unlikely to be your friends through this. They've already been brainwashed into believing that they've just struck fame and gold by discovering they're related to a brave and stunning transgender celebrity. (Because, according to the *zeitgeist*, all transgender-identified people deserve celebrity status.)

It's probably not worth expending a lot of energy on arguments about gender ideology with these extended family members, unless you think you can "peak" them — which means getting them to recognize the cult's lack of logic and wealth of lunacy — without too much effort. If you don't spend a lot of time with these people, and these relatives aren't going to be part of your protagonist village, then let sleeping dogs lie. Save your energy for more valuable conversations.

Those who aren't yet on board with this ideology or who already recognize its malevolence, merit further conversation. Get them into your village if you can.

If you're pretty sure Aunt Caroline is going to be on your side, then reach out to her and tell her what's going on. If she's local and can be an active part of your posse, so much the better. You can give her heads-up that your child is going to make this announcement, so she can have her response ready to go, as part of the strategic plan. She might say, "I'm surprised to hear this, Naomi. Gender theory doesn't hold a lot of water from what I've read. Can we sit down and talk soon? I'd really like to hear more about what you're thinking and why."

Finding a Trustworthy Therapist

A therapist is any professional who provides regular, ongoing counseling to your child or family. Different kinds of practitioners can fill this role, and any one of the following might be the right fit for your family's needs: a licensed professional counselor (LPC), a licensed marriage and family therapist (LMFT), a licensed clinical social worker (LCSW), a psychologist (Ph.D., Ed.D., or Psy.D.), a psychiatrist (M.D. or D.O.), or a pastoral counselor. Pastoral counselors may be licensed (under any of the aforementioned credentials) and practice independently. Many jurisdictions do not require counselors to be licensed when they are acting as an agent of a specific church or religious organization.

At the time of this writing, more than twenty states have passed laws that prevent counselors and therapists from doing anything other than moving a patient or client toward sex transition. Therefore, finding a gender-critical therapist who will not send your child directly to hormones and surgery can be difficult.

Be assured, there are many mental health professionals who question the claims of the gender industry and who will follow appropriate and time-tested approaches, such as investigating a child's medical, psychological, and social history, rather than slapping on a faddish label and assigning an unproven treatment protocol. But these ethical practitioners' licenses are being threatened by the current political situation around gender-identity issues in the United States, and therefore many are now flying under the radar accordingly.

If your child announces a transgender identity, how do you find a therapist you can trust?

Whether or not you're a person of religious faith, a church, temple, or mosque is a good place to start. Religious freedom is under fire by those who would see all traditional values expunged in America, but religious freedom is still the law of the land in the United States, and houses of faith still operate according to their consciences and scriptural mandates. If you know a house of worship that has not capitulated to the transgender narrative, start there. If you do not attend religious services, ask friends and colleagues about other local churches. Call the church secretary or administrator and ask about their doctrinal policy on the issue of transgenderism. If you're comfortable with the response, tell them you're looking for a therapist and you wonder if they can recommend someone.

At first, a clinical psychologist or psychiatrist may be preferred to a social worker or licensed professional counselor, as the former have more training in comprehensive diagnostic evaluations and may have more experience and better understanding of complex neurobiological syndromes than do the latter.

Vet potential therapists thoroughly. Questions to ask include:

⁜ **"Have you worked with transgender-identified patients before? How many? What were the outcomes?"**

Therapists can't discuss specific cases with you, but they should be able to tell you whether their patients desisted (stopped claiming a transgender identity) or went on to socially and/or medically transition.

A therapist can't give your child a diagnosis until after completing a full evaluation, so during your initial interview he or she won't be able to answer questions like, "Do you think my child might have [anorexia, substance abuse, et al.]?" But if your child has any other confirmed or suspected diagnoses such as autism, anorexia, social anxiety, learning disabilities, or substance abuse, you can and should ask a potential therapist, "Do you have experience working with autism (anorexia, substance abuse, etc.)?"

✢ **"What is your opinion on transgenderism/gender ideology with respect to co-occurring issues such as autism, anxiety, self-harm, prior trauma, substance abuse, and eating disorders?"**

The words *transgenderism* and *ideology* are anathema to those who accept the transgender narrative and who follow an affirmation-only approach. If you drop these words into the conversation, the therapist's response to them may tell you a great deal about their own position on the matter. Further, if the therapist does not acknowledge that significant comorbidities (two or more psychological or medical conditions that co-occur) exist between transgenderism and other neurological and emotional issues, that therapist is either undereducated on the subject of gender dysphoria, willfully ignorant, or deceptive.

✢ **"Do you think there are explanations for gender dysphoria other than being transgender?" (and/or) "Have you seen cases of gender dysphoria that were not best explained by transgenderism?"**

A good therapist should be able to name several other explanations without hesitation. If the therapist hesitates to answer these questions or struggles to answer them, that's a bad sign. The answer to both of these questions should be yes. If he or she says no, then either the therapist has virtually no experience in this area or has prejudged all gender dysphoria as being fixed transgenderism.

A good clinician will not be afraid of these questions (i.e., afraid of getting into trouble), because the "best practices" of most professional associations still encourage restraint in transgender diagnosis (at least as of this writing). If a therapist cares about scholarship and science at all, he or she will not flinch at these questions.

✠ **"What is your counseling perspective when parents and children do not agree on a course of treatment?"**

If anyone in authority in your child's life says he will "Let the child lead" or that "Children know who they really are" when you're discussing transgender ideology, run the other direction. That person has told you all you need to know. He or she will work against you, effectively wedging him- or herself as a self-designated "protector" between you and your child. Anyone who does not acknowledge that parents hold the final authority over their minor children should be kept far away from your child. If your child is an adult, however, your power to make counseling and/or medical decisions is far more limited, unfortunately. However, a good therapist should, at the very least, be willing to involve parents/guardians in the discussion.

✠ **And of course, ask about the therapist's rates and schedule, as well as what the therapist expects the duration and direction of the therapy to look like.**

Some insurance companies may provide a benefit for mental health services, but be very careful trying to save money by choosing an in-network provider who may ultimately do more harm than good. Therapy is expensive, unfortunately, and you may have to pay out-of-pocket to make sure that you have a therapist who is on your side. If you can't afford the therapist you really trust, it's worth considering that no therapy might be better than harmful therapy.

If you are dealing with an older child who has legal decision-making rights over his or her own health care but is still on your insurance, you may be able to steer the child toward a therapist of your choosing by invoking the preferred-provider clause in your insurance plan. Even if the therapist you want is not actually a preferred-provider or in-network therapist, few teens or young adults really understand how insurance policies work, so you may be able to use that pretense to exert some influence over who sees your child (without lying to your child, of course).

Finally, we would discourage you from letting your school administrators or counselors lead on this issue. The American School Counselor Association (ASCA) has put out a policy statement telling school counselors to hide from parents information about a student's gender or sexuality if the student prefers.[136] This deception underscores the lack of respect many schools now hold for parents, and while your school and/or counselor may not espouse that outlook, it's far too risky for your child and your family to offer anyone the benefit of the doubt in this situation.

Again, keep in mind that everything you do through your parenting is working toward the goal of producing a healthy and independent adult who can function positively in society and live a rewarding and productive life. The parenting that you're doing around fighting gender ideology is also in service to that goal, with the nearer-term goal of helping your child get free of the gender cult.

When he or she does, you can celebrate and sing the "Hallelujah Chorus." However, there may still be some work to be done, and we'll address that in the next chapter.

CHAPTER 7

After Desisting

*"I peaked. All those forbidden questions I kept to myself
were answered in gender critical and radical feminist groups
I joined out of curiosity. I accepted myself and my body."*

— Detransitioner who suffers from depression,
trauma, and suspected autism

"WHERE ARE YOU NOW with respect to your identity?" the mother asked. She'd had several weeks of conversations with her transgender-identified daughter, who had recently begun making critical comments about transgender ideology and some of the community that espoused it.

The teenage girl thought for a moment. "You know how when you have to go somewhere you really don't want to go, but you know you can't get out of it, because your parents are going to make you go whether you like it or not? That's how I feel about being a woman. I don't want to be female, but I realize I don't have a choice. That's what I am. So, I'm just going to work on accepting it and hope I eventually feel better about my body."

When your child desists — or gives up the belief that he or she is transgender — you may not immediately feel like celebrating. It's a strange phenomenon: sometimes when you get the thing you've most longed for and worked toward, you experience a state of disbelief, or a kind of shock. You thought you'd jump up and down for joy when it finally happened, but now you're sitting there with narrowed eyes, thinking, "Really?"

If you've experienced some of that boomeranging we discussed in the last chapter, you may fear that your child is going to flip back into gender-world over the next few days. There's no guarantee he or she won't, but preliminary reports from parents suggest that once a child makes a definitive statement ("I'm transgender" or "I'm not transgender"), the child tends to stick to that declaration with a lot of determination. It could be a factor of the black-and-white thinking that's so common to autism spectrum disorders, which are vastly overrepresented among transgender-identified people, and that causes so much difficulty getting kids out of the gender cult.

You may also feel afraid to tell other people, in case the desistance isn't "real."

That's okay.

You've just had a long, intensely challenging journey with this miserable cult and its effects on your child and family. You've likely passed through (and maybe still are passing through) some of the stages of grief.[137] You don't owe anybody a timely announcement, or any kind of information, until you're ready to give it. If you need to have a good cry, scream, and beat your fists against a tree, just sit on this news for a few weeks or months, or begin slowly by telling only the people closest to the situation, that is your right.

But even after you've finally gotten your child back, and you're ready to get on with life, you may find that he or she doesn't completely revert to being the same child you knew before. There will probably still be some work to do.

Identity

When your child abandoned the transgender narrative, the cult identity was also abandoned. But depending on how long the gender cult had your child and how old the child is, the true identity may either have been so subjugated that the child doesn't know who he or she is anymore, or the child may have matured to the point that the former identity doesn't line up with his or her chronological age.

All people who leave cults need to be reminded of who they were before; evoking parts of their true identities can be a significant step toward helping people break free from a cult's mind control. And after they're out, the work of re-becoming themselves must continue, lest they flounder and feel disconnected from themselves and from the rest of life.

The gender cult's attack on children is particularly malevolent, because children are in the process of developing their identities. If a recruit entered the gender cult at age twelve and didn't desist until he turned fifteen, he has missed a significant portion of normal, adolescent psychological and social development. He may abandon the cult identity, but his true identity may have stopped (or slowed) maturing at age twelve. Everything in his world for those three transitioned years revolved around the gender cult, and he has missed a lot of other parts of life. He knows very well that he's not a tween anymore, but he hasn't enjoyed many of the social and psychological experiences that usher most children into the middle teen years. Not only has he been sidelined; his maturation has been twisted and stunted.

One parent noted that her child began playing a certain card game again after desisting. The game had been an obsession when the child was younger, but during the gender-cult experience, the hobby was dropped. Did the child somehow revert to being who he was before he was sucked into the cult? Did he need to pick up where he left off and somehow work his way through the normal maturation process, perhaps at a faster pace?

No research exists at this time to answer these questions. Academics who have tried to study detransitioners have been largely thwarted from doing so.[138]

With respect to presentation (clothing and hairstyle choices), an informal, preliminary survey of sixty desisters and detransitioners in 2021 revealed that 47 percent continued to present their appearance the same way they did while transitioned. Only 28 percent reverted to their former appearance, and 25 percent changed to a different clothing and hairstyle but not to that of their pre-transgender identification. The study did not track how long the subjects had been detransitioned, nor was a follow-up study ever pursued. (See Appendix B.)

What might be keeping so many desisters and detransitioners "stuck" in their cult presentation, even after they've left the cult? Cult-created fears could provide a clue.

Cult-Created Fears

Fear is a powerful motivator. Like many cults, the gender cult uses fear to keep gender-confused people in line with the cult narrative. By training its members that they are only safe when they are inside the cult community and abiding by its rules, cults instill fears that may linger long after the member has left the ideology. Until the fears are dealt with, the member may not fully recover his or her true identity.[139]

Many of us have arachnophobia, which means we are terrified of spiders. I know logically that spiders are good, because they control the insect population; I know they are more scared of me than I am of them; I know that most spiders are not harmful to humans, or interested in biting me or having anything at all to do with me. Yet when I notice one near me, I panic: I instinctively scramble to distance myself while at the same time flailing my arms to try to fling the object of my terror far away from me. I nearly wrecked my car once, when I folded down my sun visor and found a large spider clinging to it, inches from my face.

The gender cult inculcates in its recruits a number of different fears.[140] Some of these may include:

- ✣ fear of those outside the gender cult, who are painted as toxic, hateful, bigoted, and dangerous.

- ✣ fear of adulthood: puberty blockers are touted as the only way to prevent passing through puberty, which may force you into "the wrong kind" of adulthood. The very idea of growing up and becoming responsible for oneself may induce fear as well.

- ✣ fear of one's own sex or sexuality. Girls may be terrified of being vulnerable to unwanted attention from predatory men. Boys may fear they don't measure up as men or will never be able to attract a mate.

- ✣ fear of being homosexual. If the child experiences what he or she thinks is same-sex attraction, great discomfort can accompany those feelings, especially if the family doesn't approve of homosexuality.

- ✣ fear of not having the same sexual feelings that peers seem to be experiencing. If kids experience delayed puberty, or their sex drives don't seem to be matching those of other kids their age (who are likely over-sexed anyway, because of our culture's saturation with all things sexual), they may believe that something about them is inherently broken.

✢ fear of being victimized. The gender industry teaches people that they are inherently victims of society if others do not celebrate everything about them and their beliefs. People who have already suffered trauma may have firsthand experience with victimization, and they've been even further indoctrinated with the expectation that they will continue to be victimized if they don't transition sexes.

✢ fear of lacking control over oneself and others. When a person announces a transgender identity, suddenly he or she is granted complete power over other people: everyone must respond a certain way, use the preferred name and pronouns, as well as affirm and approve of everything the transgender-identified person says and does. Social and medical transition can also give a sense of control: *I can remake myself any way I want to be.* Turning one's back on gender ideology may feel like giving up complete control over one's life.

✢ fear of being unkind or intolerant. Gender ideology has ridden into town on the back of equity-diversity-inclusion doctrine, successfully convincing people that to question anything about the transgender narrative is to be inherently hateful and bigoted. People who have recognized the fallacies in the doctrine may still be emotionally programmed to think they are heretics if they disagree with it. This is a classic example of cognitive dissonance, or holding two opposing beliefs at the same time. It is very common to hear detransitioners caveat their stories by saying that they don't mean to question or take away from any "true trans" people's experiences.

⛨ fear of being targeted by their former communities. People who detransition often find themselves and their experiences denigrated by the very community who celebrated and glorified them when they identified as transgender. Detransitioners are told they were "never trans in the first place" and that they've become "TERFs."[141]

Because research into detransitioners and their experiences is so sparse at the time of this writing, it's very difficult to pinpoint how many and what sort of fears may have been instilled into transgender-identified people by the gender industry. Many more may exist than are catalogued here.

Continue to talk with your child about his or her experiences with the transgender community before, during, and after transgender identification, as the topic emerges organically or via subtle leading. (Detransitioners often complain that their parents talked about little but transgender ideology.) Ask open-ended questions to probe what fears may still linger, or what is occupying your child's thoughts now:

> "Is there anything that scares you about life or about
> the future?"
> "What do you think your life will be like five years
> from now?
> "If you could change one thing about the world, what
> would it be?"

Treatments to overcome fears, such as exposure therapy, cognitive behavior therapy, and mindfulness training, can be very effective.[142] If the fears are somewhat mild and don't significantly impair a person's day-to-day life, professional therapy may not be necessary in order to deal with and/or overcome these fears. A few strategies may help you guide your child out of fears that he or she adopted as a result of gender cult indoctrination.

FACTS VS. REALITY

Simply recognizing that a fear has no basis in reality may be all that's necessary to alleviate it. The gender cult's insistence that people outside the transgender community are dangerous and toxic is one of the easiest to disprove, especially if you have successfully guided your child away from the cult by liberal administrations of love and truth. Pointing out that people like J. K. Rowling have been incredibly supportive of the transgender community but were scathingly vilified simply for expressing a question or concern about some aspect of it, plainly reveals the deception and underhandedness of the cult's own toxicity.[143]

Examine with your child some of his or her experiences with the transgender cult and community. Your child may continue to express certain beliefs that were drilled into recruits, such as "Transgender people are being killed at alarming rates" (which is untrue).[144] Ask gentle but probing questions, such as "Where did you hear that? What support do you have for that statement, such as crime statistics or research data?" Your child will start to question other things that the gender cult taught as well.

LOCUS OF CONTROL[145]

A disturbing trend in education and childrearing today encourages children to view themselves as helpless victims of other's actions. Kids are taught that everyone is either oppressed or an oppressor, that they need to have "safe spaces," and that anything they find uncomfortable is a "trigger" that needs to be avoided.[146]

This perspective on negotiating life fundamentally changes a person's *locus of control* from *internal* to *external*. That's a significant problem for a number of reasons.

A person who possesses an *internal locus of control* believes that he or she has control over his or her own life. These people tend to take responsibility for themselves and their actions, they believe that their choices drive their life outcomes, and they usually have fairly high self-esteem as well as a good work ethic. They tend to be happier and healthier overall than people whose locus of control is outside of themselves.

A person with an *external locus of control* believes that he or she is helpless against others' whims and megrims. People who believe that they do not have the power to make changes to their lives, or to have any effect on the world, think that they can only react to what happens to them. They blame others or they blame situations for their circumstances, and they generally feel powerless and hopeless about their futures. They tend not to be productive employees or confident people, because they don't equate hard work or good decisions with success. They credit (bad) luck for everything.

Maintaining an external locus of control undermines one's personal well-being and society's ultimate good. But gender ideology is all about the external locus of control:

✠ "You don't have a choice about your gender identity; it's how you were born."

✠ "You feel bad about yourself and about life because of the way others treat you."

✠ "Others' words can make you suicidal."

✠ "You have to be protected from anything and anyone who makes you uncomfortable."

✠ "Uncomfortable feelings must be excised with drugs and surgery."

If you recognize that your desisted child still expresses an external locus of control about his or her life and future, talk through some of those beliefs and help guide your child toward an internal locus of control:

✠ "You can't choose your sex, but you can decide what kind of personality you want to express, and what sort of activities you prefer to do."

✠ "What others do may hurt, but you can decide that their words say more about them than they do about you. Maybe they're just jerks. That's not your problem."

✠ "Others' words can hurt or disappoint us, but we can choose to ignore them, and listen to our own voices, and to the voices of those who we know are honest and who love us."

✠ "Being uncomfortable is a prerequisite for growth and maturity. You can't get stronger, for example, without exercising and breaking down muscles so they can be rebuilt more powerfully."

✠ "Uncomfortable feelings are just red flags to help us sort through things that we might need to change in our lives."

TALK THERAPY

A major part of talk therapy is simply asking questions and letting the other person verbally work through what's troubling him or her. If your child has remnants of fears left over from the cult, a few pertinent questions might help him or her to verbalize those ideas, and move past them:

✛ "What's the worst thing that could happen if you meet up with someone who is actually transphobic?"

✛ "What are some things you could do if you got to college and realized something about it was too hard for you to handle?"

✛ "What might a good response be if someone tells you that you were never 'really trans' in the first place? Do you need to respond to that at all?"

Loss of Community and Resources

Be sensitive to the fact that when a person leaves the gender cult, significant losses occur. The desister/detransitioner has lost the entire community of gender ideologues and allies, as well as all the encouragement, adulation, and support that accompanies that community. Healthcare providers and therapists who subscribe to affirmation-only have nothing to offer people who realize that affirmation-only did not serve their real needs. If the child experienced medicalization via hormones or surgery, the doctors who provided those physical interventions have limited, if any, ability to restore or reverse the changes that the patient no longer wants; those doctors may also behave defensively if they fear being accused of malpractice. The financial, legal, and advocacy resources that pro-transgender organizations may have provided suddenly disappear.[147] One detransitioner poignantly explains this deep loss:

> When you detransition, you give up a lot. You're basically announcing to the world, "Hey, I made a mistake." So you're humiliated, and you also end up losing a lot of friends and losing a lot of your community and losing

resources.... When you're detransitioning you're going through the process of addressing your trauma. You're addressing these mental health issues finally, for the first time, sometimes in a long time. So you're going through the process of exiting out of the community you've been a part of, exiting out of this identity, this life you've been a part of for so long, and exiting this world where now you've got all of this baggage. And you need someone to talk about it [with], and you need someone who's going to care about your health, who is willing to understand there might be long-term health consequences to what you did, and [who will] be able to help you through that. Unfortunately, we don't really have those resources right now.[148]

Restoration

Your child succumbed to the gender cult because something about it fed a perceived need. As he or she becomes healthier and more stable in the weeks and months after leaving the cult, you might consider asking what made gender ideology appealing. Assessing, along with your child, whether the vulnerability is still there may help you and your child sort out the long-term goal of the child achieving healthy, secure, and productive independence as an adult.

If necessary, please forgive your child for the trouble and trauma that this season almost certainly brought into your lives. People who come out of the gender cult often blame themselves, both for having gotten sucked into it and for the damage that was wrought on their bodies by drugs and/or surgeries. Both you and your child need to place the blame for this debacle squarely where it belongs: on the unethical and predatory gender industry, and the activism machine that has driven it into every corner of society.

Everyone is susceptible to cult indoctrination to some degree. Where does motivation theory leave off and undue influence begin? When are we being encouraged and when does encouragement cross the line into manipulation? What is the difference between healthy practices devoted to developing self-discipline and growth, versus abusive practices that diminish, gaslight, or control us?

If you haven't done so already (or haven't done so for a while), assure your child that you are on his or her side, that you love him or her, and that you are committed to giving all the support necessary for full healing. Spend quality time doing enjoyable activities together. Laugh together. Cry together. Make sure that your child feels fully restored to relationship with the family.

An interesting trend about family closeness has emerged from a preliminary survey of desisters and detransitioners. In most cases, from both the child's and parent's perspectives, the child's relationship with the parents was perceived to take a dive during the time the child was in the gender cult. However, in most cases, the relationship was either restored to the same level of closeness *or higher* after the child left the cult. This trend holds whether the relationship was perceived as excellent or poor prior to the transition. The relationship nearly always improved by the end of the journey. This is an incredibly promising and hopeful outcome. (See Appendix B for more details about this survey and its results.)

This calamitous cultural phenomenon — when children are taught, encouraged, and pressured to attempt to change sexes — will come to an end eventually. Gender identity is the medical scandal of the twenty-first century, akin to the lobotomy debacle of the mid-twentieth century and the repressed-memories craze of the 1980s and 1990s. This cult's ideology is based on misinformation and disinformation, and will crumble at some point, because truth always comes to light.

Until the demise of gender theory, however, vulnerable children will continue to be sucked in and abused by this unethical industry. But families needn't blindly capitulate to the industry's demands. All roads do not lead to the gender clinic. We can parent our children with real love and durable truth, keeping or getting our sons and daughters away from the gender cult.

As more and more children grow up, wake up, and confront horror and regret over what's been done to them, they will begin to ask all the adults who should've been safeguarding them, "Why did this happen? Why didn't someone stop me?"

May our children never be among them.

Copublisher's Note

ADVOCATES PROTECTING CHILDREN COMMENDS parents who seek out the truth about gender ideology and the gender industry, and who strive to protect their children from this nefarious, profit-driven machine. You are doing difficult, important, and compassionate work, and you deserve more partners and better support than you may have experienced as you fight a cultural tsunami that preys upon vulnerable children and vilifies good and loving parents. We salute you.

If Advocates Protecting Children can be of any service or help to you, please reach out to us:

www.advocatesprotectingchildren.org
advocatesprotectingchildren@gmail.com

Please also visit the Resources section of this book to find organizations and support for pushing back against the gender industry, in your home and in the culture.

You are not alone. More and more people are recognizing the atrocities being perpetrated in the name of gender-affirming medicine. In the months and years to come Advocates Protecting Children fully expects to see this diabolical industry taken down. We wish you every success in safeguarding your family as all adults of conscience work to end the unethical medicalization of our precious children.

In Their Own Words: Messages from Desisters/ Detransitioners

Taken from a survey of desisted/detransitioned people, and of parents who have walked through this journey with their children, the following quotes are meant to encourage, inspire, caution, and inform parents who may be just starting out on this journey or who are looking for a new direction to try to help their children.

Quotes are taken directly from the survey and edited very lightly for grammar, brevity, or clarity, when necessary. Some of the advice and commentary you will read here conflicts with other advice and commentary, and with that given elsewhere in this book. A few of the comments may come from younger children, as well.

Caveat emptor.

What Should Parents Do?

"Don't push [your child] away. The reason I never told my parents is because I know they would have disagreed and called me crazy, which would have strengthened my position against them and caused me to find a new 'family' who would accept my identity. Just be there for them."

"Do not try to limit your child's wishes to change things that ultimately don't matter. Hair, clothes, pronouns, activities (like hobbies), a name — all that is temporary. Restricting your child there will just make them resent and not trust you. Besides, your child should be able to control their look anyway."

"Give your child autonomy outside of the medical sphere. Your child, if identifying as trans, inherently will not trust you. You need to show you can be trusted. Refusing medical intervention needs to be [concerned with the] medical impact, not in how it would change the kid's look — they want those changes. Don't fearmonger about regret. Just [sharing] the reasons, [like the] lack of research on the effects [and dangers] for growing bodies needs to be enough. A binder is a hard spot to walk because the kid may really want it but they're far less healthy than the trans community describes. Try to frame that refusal that way as well and find a different way for the kid to make her chest appear flat. It's all about letting the kid have control over her life without hurting herself. She may still resent you and she may still go on to transition after turning eighteen, but there's a much better chance she *will* trust you, and that she will see your concerns as grounded in love for her not the idea of her as a girl. That is key."

"Question how the child came to this conclusion and reinforce that the child is perfect the way they are, they don't need to change anything to prove anything to anyone. Say that liking things about being the opposite sex doesn't make you trans, and you can perfectly be cis and dress and act the way you want because being women or men isn't defined by clothes or actions."

"Stay calm but educate the child about the matter. Let them know the realities of gender transitioning. Seek help from a nonconforming counselor or therapist."

"Don't encourage/affirm it at all and find a therapist who deals with body dysmorphia/eating disorders that can help the person be comfortable in their body the way it is."

"Hold firm boundaries. I used to say, 'I know you believe you are a boy; that must be hard. But I don't believe that.' Pick your battles. Hair grows, clothes can change, but monitor Internet use and discourage binding."

"Stay strong in the truth that trans is an inauthentic identity."

"Affirm their identity while blocking them from irreversible changes. They are crying out to be seen and heard. The parent must provide this in order to show the child that they are on their team. In a nurturing environment, the child will be free to reflect on themselves and their truth. More importantly, the trans community encourages people to cut off their parents if the parents challenge the identity. Cultrecovery101.com even says that family should show an interest in the cult and support the victim carefully in order to show that you are on their side, lest they cut you off and surrender to the cult. To help remove them from it, share your own interests and bits of the real world. Challenge their beliefs in a nonthreatening way."

"Remove their online influences, find a therapist who is *not* affirming, homeschool or otherwise change the child's environment, enroll them in body-positive physical activities."

"Talk to the child about misogyny, let the child express her thoughts on what it's like to meet the world as a female, validation and support. Avoid referring to womanhood as something negative (trivializing emotions: 'must be on her period,' 'X throws like a girl'). Highlight the child's abilities and skills, acknowledge her personality; focus on her inner traits, avoid vanity. Focus on self-expression rather than transition."

"Maintain relationship without affirming. Validate feelings but not beliefs."

"At least one parent needs to keep communication channels open and slowly introduce evidence that helps the child question gender ideology."

"Allow experimentation with clothing and other expression without gendering those things. Introduce positive gender-nonconforming role models. Explain that gender is only what society tells you and you don't have to participate."

"Pray more, love more, affirm feelings, speak the *truth* (don't affirm ideology), restrict Internet use, pray even more..."

"Affirm the child's feelings, listen, do not judge or deny the child's point of view, and in return for helping social transitioning, try to help the child to see the benefit of waiting for medical procedures until they are older — especially the more intrusive and irreversible ones. Always show the child support and let them know that they can always change their mind at any point in their journey."

"Try to be calm, try to maintain a relationship where the child knows he or she is still loved. He or she is most likely being highly coached by other transgenders, and is attracted to being accepted and having a new life 'purpose.' We told our son we would not be able to 'affirm or celebrate' his transgender ideas, but we would compromise the best we could (for which we were continually told there is no compromise). Compromise to us meant gender-neutral clothing in our presence (jeans, T-shirt, sweatshirt, etc.). We would call him 'honey,' 'dear,' 'you,' etc., but not his legally changed name. That was unacceptable to him, so he was estranged for long periods at a time. I didn't want him to be hungry, so I'd occasionally send him gift cards to food stores; I would not give him money because I knew he'd spend it on hormones or makeup. It was very hard to know what to do; we were heartbroken and desperate for him to stop. He was an adult, so we had no choice in his hormones. If he was a minor, I'd never let myself be bullied into authorizing or paying for hormones. But these days, it's almost impossible to stop a minor from getting hormones. In good conscience, I'd not let myself be party to it though."

"I explained that she could never actually change sex and while I would always support her I didn't want her to do anything that could not be undone. She didn't ask for a different name/pronoun."

"Genuine love, respect, and conversations about the child's life choices."

"Be supportive of the child and do not abandon them, but be robust in opposing the ideology."

"My mother was extremely firm about me being a woman and would have never entertained me being anything else. She never once budged — but this was probably easier for her because she is a very religious immigrant more concerned with acceptance from her religious/immigrant community that doesn't care about gender ideology. I do think it would've been harder if she was an American concerned with acceptance from other Americans who've embraced gender ideology, if that makes sense. As firm as she was, she also no longer brings up or harps on that period in my life now that it's over, which has helped our relationship so much because I am very embarrassed about ever thinking I was nonbinary and she doesn't have a grudge about it.

Since then, we've been able to connect over being women even though she's a super religious straight woman and I'm a lesbian."

"Be loving but firm. Never be angry or dismissive or judgmental, but be firm."

"Be gentle. Let them discover who they are but do not take them to an affirm-only therapist. Find a reputable psychiatrist and a reputable [family] therapist. Limit and monitor their social media intake. Slowly introduce evidence of biological reality. Try to understand where they're coming from and let them have their identity but make sure if it's just a phase, they haven't harmed their body with Lupron and surgery."

"Introduce them to radical feminism and show how transient discomfort does not mean that you must change yourself so radically."

"Understand that children are being exposed to inappropriate content earlier than ever, and that content often dehumanizes women. Eliminate access to that content."

"Try to find out with the child what the actual reasons for the child's discomfort with their body, sex, gender roles, name, pronouns, etc. are."

"My parents didn't judge me when I started transitioning and they didn't judge me when I detransitioned. I don't regret my journey and I'm glad they were supportive of me the entire time."

"I think the single most important thing is to attempt to remain loving and yet set some real boundaries and not be afraid to seek help early."

"Our church was crucial."

"Discuss with the child. Let them speak their mind and explain why they feel this way. Listen to what they say, and offer advice and other explanations as to why they may be feeling this way. Let them know you love them and want them to be happy."

"Honestly affirming the child while not condoning it. The more a parent tries to constrain a child's ability to express themselves, the more the child will act out. I think there has to be a balance."

What Should Parents Not Do?

"Rejecting the child outright is a bad idea."

"Don't restrict your kid into a gendered box. That's part of what causes dysphoria in the first place. Don't frame transition as bad because it's regrettable or masculinizing. Don't latch on to the idea of your child as a girl rather than the idea of your child — they can sniff that out and they *won't* trust you because they can tell you value the idea of them more than them regardless of how they look and act. This doesn't mean acquiescing to everything. It means being understanding of your child and giving them safe, supported freedom to explore nonconformity."

"No surgeries [or] hormones."

"Getting angry. The child will likely become more fixated on the idea of transitioning if you deny their idea aggressively."

"Don't affirm with name or pronouns."

"Don't stop an open line of communication. Talk to your kid about their feelings and don't push back but don't affirm either. Don't take away their friends either."

"Trying to argue or browbeat the child. I did it and it failed. Once I was calm but clear and consistent, it helped."

"Don't use the new name and pronouns — they need to remain grounded in reality!"

"No medical intervention without several years of therapy, and none before a consenting adult age. Don't talk out your worries with them, seek support from a third party. Don't tell them they're just crazy or the devil is making them think they're trans, don't try to convince them they're not trans."

"You are fighting against a cult mindset and affirmation is never the right answer."

"Do not outright deny the child's identity, but also don't blindly affirm everything without question."

"Be supportive of his or her emotional journey in this time of self-discovery."

"Any affirmation; seeking untrustworthy professionals."

"Our biggest mistake was not screening the first psychologist we sent our daughter to."

"Not allowing them to explore gender identity at all."

"Turning the situation into a war with the parent and child on opposite sides."

"Yelling and arguing accomplishes nothing. They think they are 100 percent correct in everything they say about transgender. And parents know nothing. You want them to stop immediately, but in reality there are things they have to learn for themselves, and often learned through bad experience and pain. You can make them more determined to be transgender if you fight them. But we said no money or affirmation of ours would go towards something we did not believe in."

"Every child is different; I think I just got lucky that mine came out the other end unharmed. I would hesitate to affirm too strongly as it could be too difficult for the child to change their mind."

"Attacking a child's choices, making them feel guilty for feelings they cannot control, comparing hormone usage (which the child believes is a genuine medical treatment) to drug abuse."

"Believing it when you have doubts."

"Abandoning them to a *de facto* cult."

"Indulging the fantasy only strengthens it."

"Don't base their entire life and worth about gender ideology. Try to build a supportive community around your kid but don't make it all about being trans."

"Don't become preachy, these kids want radical acceptance and attention, not more dogma."

"Do not affirm under any circumstances. Don't insult, but never bend reality for the child."

"Don't obsess over the 'transness' in an overly positive *or* negative way."

"Don't do individual therapy for the child — make therapy a family situation. There is no reason to trust that a therapist is going to be fair and neutral and support a strong family, so the parent has to force that issue."

"No unsupervised time with friends/relatives who may undermine you."

"Shaming your child will only lead to pain. There is a reason your child feels this way, try to find the source. Is it body image issues? Discomfort with gender roles? Is there genuine dysphoria? Are they bored? It is extremely difficult as a parent to see your child go through this, but it's important to not be against your child. It should be parent and child vs. whatever is making your child feel bad, not parent vs. child."

"Trying to make the child feel bad or completely being unsupportive."

"Sending videos and articles as to why gender ideology is wrong and generally trying to convince them that they don't know themselves."

On Therapists

"I had a normal counselor who thought I was trans because I purposely dropped hints about my dysphoria rather than talking about it directly. I found out quite later that she also thought I may be autistic. I also had a gender therapist for one Skype appointment who gave me a dysphoria diagnosis."

"To be honest I was doing therapy because I have major depression and anxiety, the trans part was something that we talked about but wasn't the center point."

"The therapist wasn't knowledgeable about trans matters. She said so herself, but affirmed anyway."

"We did not talk about transgender identity. We addressed underlying issues. We have a conversion therapy ban in our state."

"The mental health team spent most of our joint sessions trying to get me to affirm.... My daughter had been raped.... I said this may be a trauma response. I was told she had been transgender from ... three years old, but I had just refused to see it. We are currently trying to get her trauma counseling."

"I wanted to bring up the issue in therapy so many times, but I was terrified she would confirm this meant I was trans. I was worried about 'speaking it into being,' I suppose you could say."

"The psychologist was like [a] brainwasher, who told the child to be transgender. Psychology was the driving force. Psychology is not scientific, and is very dangerous."

"The sole gender specialist I saw lied about or made up studies and statistics, seemed to regard me as entertainment instead of a person with a problem, talked about her personal interests in Ru Paul as well as her other clients, tried convincing my husband that he was a trans woman when I brought him in to process our disagreements over my transition, and through it all somehow managed to convince me that I was FTM [female to male transgender]. The reactions among other therapists were mixed, but all were professional."

"The counselor was a personal friend of my father's and maybe as a result I never opened up to her about my real traumas and she didn't dig deep enough."

"The 'gender specialist' asked my twelve-year-old about fetishes and BDSM [bondage, domination, sadism, and masochism] sex, and pushed for surgery."

"We were not comfortable with the first psychologist, and felt we were deceived to put our trust in this person 'helping' our son since it seemed to do more harm than good. The second psychologist we trusted much more, but due to privacy issues we did not know much. We paid for both psychologists."

"Therapy was arranged via the school."

"They disapproved of my doubts that my child was trans."

"In retrospect it felt like indoctrination."

"I dropped the question once, about gender dysphoria and the like, but she never resumed the topic and I left before I truly desisted."

"We saw several therapists, including social workers in various hospitalization and treatment programs. Only *one* was clear that our daughter had deeper issues than a trans identity and she would focus on working on *those* issues rather than the identity. Every other therapist was all-in on the only issue being the trans identity. We fired a number of therapists, or had barely-functioning non-aggressive agreements."

On Reasons for Desisting/Detransitioning

"I peaked. All those forbidden questions I kept to myself were answered in gender critical and radical feminist groups I joined out of curiosity. I accepted myself and my body; I can be and look 'boyish' and still be a woman."

"I came out as lesbian."

"Surgery pain, near-death experience."

"I do not know why my dysphoria desisted. I'm assuming it's a combination of age and the fact that I actually handled it pretty well after transitioning. (Transitioning only can alleviate dysphoria, not get rid of it, so I still had to develop coping strategies, and I got good at it.)"

"I saw the suffering of my mom, so I started to question if I really was [transgender] because my whole life I dressed and acted as a boy but was I really trans just because of this? At the time I started seeing women who identify as women and had the same dysphoria as I had. Seeing that I could be a woman and be whatever I wanted [showed me that] was possible. Of course, I have to deal with homophobia now, but I'm pretty fine the way I am."

"I think mostly it was being away from influences at school and off the Internet."

"I had a depressive episode and started trying to heal myself and realized I didn't need to be a man to be comfortable in life."

"She was more alone, and rejected by people who thought she was mentally ill."

"I realized I had been lied to about many things, especially science, politics."

"Posie Parker's 'adult human female' campaign snapped me out of my gender haze because I realized womanhood really is that simple. It has nothing to do with 'feeling like a woman,' a concept I had wrestled with for years. Gender Critical Reddit and radical feminist blogs/articles/videos helped me to process what I'd been through, as I felt so alone in this gender questioning, OCD thought-spiral for so long. Knowing it's widespread throughout young millennials (I was born in 1996) and Gen Z helped me to have compassion for myself and not feel so stupid. A lot of us got sucked in."

"Faith in the ideology slowly fell apart over the course of a year as all of the above [reasons listed in the survey], as well as self-reflection, took place. Pandemic isolation also played a huge role, feeling comfortable as I am in the absence of social pressure."

"I think it had a lot to do with her current boyfriend, who likes girls, and he always treated her as a girl. He refused to affirm her, but wanted to date her."

"We had many discussions about critically thinking about what was going on given that many of the girls on her year level were transgender or gender fluid."

"She began to realize her transgender ideology was a way to cope with severe anxiety."

"They began to be concerned about how trans activists refused any discussion that deviated from the medical transition route. They also decided that surgery was unlikely to 'fix' the dysphoria they felt and decided they would rather seek treatment to help them deal with the root cause of dysphoria. They are now awaiting confirmation of a diagnosis of [Borderline Personality Disorder]."

"It was a gradual process. After six years of hormones and life-style, he came off the hormones cold turkey. It seemed to make him feel physically 'better' but not immediately. He was not under the care of a physician. His clothing and hairstyle also changed over many months as if he was mentally preparing to appear male again. He has been detransitioned for over three years. He appears male, and works a physically hard blue-collar job which he loves. He does not want to talk about his time being transgender female."

"She hated puberty and feeling she was typically 'girly,' as she always preferred short hair and jeans, and hated makeup. She spent a lot of time on the Internet and was told she must be trans in that case."

"I started to miss the fellowship I had with women when I was read as one. This played a part in me considering my parents' arguments."

"She fell out of love with a gay guy, and into love with a straight guy."

"Through maturing in my late 20s, I came to see how insisting upon puffing up an artificial reality was holding me back. I took on a practice of radical acceptance and started over."

"I realized that it was extremely unethical, to myself, and others. My body is not profane [sic] and suitable for mutilation and modification to assuage my mind."

"Grew out of dysphoria and became at ease with being lesbian."

"[He] realized [his] obsession with being female came about from watching pornography."

"She was not allowed to use her 'identity' to control other people. The therapist in her first residential program simply gave her an opportunity to disclose that she was trans and our daughter did not. Then, after a week or so, our kid said, 'Well, I'm trans,' so she wouldn't have to do anything (which was her M.O.) and the attention would shift to everything being *our* issues to solve. The therapist said, 'I gave you a chance — in fact, our entire first two sessions — to declare what you felt were the issues which needed to be addressed. Springing something new is negatively manipulating. We'll only be working on the stuff you identified, not throwing out a wide net.' [The therapist] also hammered that a family sending a kid away for treatment means there are serious, massive issues which are intractable and can't be handled by a traditional therapist in a suburban office setting. And that she had much deeper, more serious things to work on than controlling our family, which was going to be a losing strategy because her troublesome behaviors were alienating us from her."

Do Other Health/Psychological Issues Exist?

"The autism is at most a maybe and could be ADHD [Attention-Deficit/Hyperactivity Disorder] instead, it's hard to tell as I'm rather functional. Another big factor alongside depression was my anxiety, which I now think may be OCD [obsessive-compulsive disorder]."

"[My child] may have inherited trauma from me."

"Anxiety and PTSD [Post-Traumatic Stress Disorder]"

"Dyslexia and dyscalculia, plus her father is bipolar and was confusing and became emotionally abusive after disclosure.... We separated at this time."

"I was depressed around ages 8/9 and 12/13 but developing ROGD [Rapid-Onset Gender Dysphoria] at 16 plunged me into my worst and longest depressive period. (Still working to break out of the bad coping mechanisms I developed as a result, LOL!)"

"Homosexuality"

"Dissociative Identity Disorder, Eating Disorder"

"Sexual molestation by female peer, bullying, early puberty with extreme discomfort"

"ADHD, social anxiety"

"Anxiety and some sensory issues since childhood"

"High school was very socially challenging, and he struggled to fit in."

"Her first relationship was very controlling, and the boyfriend was charged by police."

"Fear of pregnancy"

"ADHD, undiagnosed"

"I would note that our daughter had a fight response to anxiety or perceived threat. Meanwhile, her father had a fight response as well, and her mother (me) and her sisters have a freeze response. This led to our daughter physically assaulting *everyone* in the immediate family and also, long-term, being verbally and emotionally abusive."

"Mild trichotillomania" (hair-pulling/plucking)

A Final Word

"I'm just glad I was an adult when it happened. If I was younger, and growing up now, I'm sure I'd have gone further. I wanted to be a boy very much when I was a kid."

"Ultimately you cannot and should not treat this as something to train your child out of. Children are their own people. You can't do that. It will only create resentment. They will not trust you and they will hate you. They will just keep everything secret and disappear as soon as they can upon becoming adults. Instead, just draw lines around medical risk from a place of support. Try your best to support their exploration in safe ways. It is only with support in their autonomy that they may realize they can be how they want regardless of identity. Preaching to them doesn't help, it just makes them not trust you."

"This person most probably used trans as a coping mechanism for dealing with intense stress. After the situation alleviated, they began feeling the opposite and regretted transitioning."

"I think it was for attention and popularity."

"My daughter, now 17, is doing better in school. She doesn't self-harm and she has a boyfriend. She would describe herself as a TERF [trans-exclusionary radical feminist] with pride. She refers to this period in her life as 'when I was unwell.' She is very clear how influenced she was by social media and has changed her use of it."

"I transitioned during a time when I was feeling powerful and coming into myself, but I also felt like the rules had changed and I was told a lot of lies in order to convert me. I don't know what's reality anymore, so I'm trying to figure it out. I feel brainwashed. I think I might be a gender nonconforming woman who likes women. That may be why a cross-gender presentation and inclusion in the LGBT population made me feel happy and free."

"I recommend that the parent gets as much support as they can for themselves. It can feel like a real lonely time but you'll soon discover there are many families going through the same thing. Talk to friends. Get counseling for yourself. I recommend a psychologist that has been in the field for at least two decades (ideally more). And most importantly make it very clear to your child's teachers that they are not to affirm — making a point to say that the child is in therapy trying to work out what is really going on. I sent the school lots of information to support our goal of not affirming."

"My child explains when they were around twelve they started to feel unhappy at the sexualization of females and didn't identify with a lot of the female images they were presented with in the mainstream media, and at the time their dress sense was pretty androgynous and they didn't have many female friends. They were active on Tumblr at the time and when they aired their concerns about how they didn't feel completely aligned with the female gender they feel they were 'groomed' by the Tumblr community into transitioning as a 'cure' for these feelings."

"So hard. So painful. Our son started pre-Bruce Jenner, so many friends and acquaintances did not realize how prevalent transgender was becoming. We felt stigmatized and like we were bad parents. You can't tell a minor or adult child to 'just stop.' It doesn't work that way, but others think you can. Some people thought it was funny, and it's very embarrassing. It was hard to talk about. I felt like we were living two lives — one for people who did not know what we were going through, and another with the few friends who knew our anguish. It's nearly impossible to not talk about an adult child with those who don't know, as other parents see their children finish college, get married, established, etc., and yours is struggling in so many ways just to survive."

"I truly believe social media is to blame for this. My daughter was told that if she didn't fit into the stereotypical girl mold, she was a boy."

"People at my college want to kill me for being detrans."

"She tells me she was swept along with the fashion, including some cutting. This was in 2008–2009. She is horribly embarrassed by it all now. I am not, but respect her privacy."

"I went through my whole adventure before it became a cultural phenomenon. I was alone for the most part, and my common sense was always there, nagging at me. Even as a teen, I logically knew there was probably nothing anyone could do to make me a boy, unless I got my own fairy godmother. I learned early that I couldn't control how people saw me and figured it was probably fascist to try. It took me ages to figure out why the inside didn't seem to match the outside. People assumed things about me based on my body that aren't true. When everyone assumes the same wrong things, this gets extremely disorienting. A less timid temperament, especially in the current climate, it's easy to believe I would have taken more permanent steps. And although I stopped presenting outwardly after a few years, I thought of myself as secretly a man inside for roughly 15 years, circa 1997 to 2012."

"Being a semi-open desister, and being very critical of trans ideology, can paint a huge target on one's back, a modern-day pariah in 'woke and progressive' circles. It can be tough to self-silence to avoid the ravenous mob hurling 'transphobia' and the hypocrisy as they campaign to invalidate your lived experience. But being authentic, and imperfectly human, has been worth it, thousands of times over."

"We heard through friends/family that our son detransed, but he hasn't spoken to us since moving out and won't return our calls, so all answers are to the best of my knowledge (secondhand)."

"I know that our family's experience is probably an outlier. Our daughter became physical and violent (and she was violent with treatment staff, as well). She controlled and threatened her sisters *before* she seemed to have an identity fixation. Because of the nature of being the targets of abuse from a child, I would say our relationship is OK, but I'm not sure it will *ever* be close, because it was so destructive. She told lies about us — that we were abusing her. She lives across the country. I talk to her often, but it's surface-level. I love her, but I don't trust her. I have never spoken to her about the trans-identification because I am loath to dive back into that and have to re-experience it. I am diagnosed with chronic PTSD [post-traumatic stress disorder] over the entire situation. I continue to feel misled and mistreated by the mental health professions."

"I think having to start aggressively defending myself at every given moment at home left very little space for me to experiment with my gender identity — it in itself solidified my gender identity very early on. If I had a more open environment to experiment with being gender-nonconforming, I might have reached a different conclusion."

Data from Partners for Ethical Care's 2021 Desister/ Detransitioner Survey

INCLUDED HERE ARE THE questions and aggregate responses from an informal and preliminary survey given to people who have desisted (stopped insisting they do not identify with their birth sex) and/or detransitioned (stopped attempting to change sexes and/or present one's appearance differently than his or her birth sex), and to parents of desisters/detransitioners, during the month of February 2021.[149]

This is a very small, non-randomized and self-selected sample of sixty people who submitted their responses with the opportunity to do so anonymously; thirty respondents provided contact information and thirty did not. *Results must be considered with caution*, because of the small sample size, because the sample is not a random selection from the pool of desisters/detransitioners, and because of the lack of authentication and adequate demographic data on the respondents. If this survey reveals anything, it strongly suggests that more rigorous research is needed on the phenomenon of desisting/ detransitioning.

Partners for Ethical Care feels confident that all sixty responses included in these results are genuine. Approximately thirty-five additional responses were submitted and subsequently removed. These responses were recognized as disingenuous or invalid by several criteria:

1. the respondent commented, "I'm just here to mess up your data";

2. the respondent left disparaging, silly, and/or crude comments;

3. the respondent entered multiple, identical survey submissions; and/or

4. the respondent gave contradictory information, such as ticking every box in response to Question 13, "Which of the following did the parent do after the child announced a transgender identity?" including "The parent did nothing different."

If a survey submission met any of the above criteria, it was removed. One additional survey submission was removed because the parent who submitted it indicated that the child had not yet desisted or detransitioned.

Most questions were answered by all sixty respondents. The percentages listed beneath some questions may or may not sum to 100 percent, depending on whether the question could only be answered with a single response, or if the question included a "Check all that apply" option. Unless otherwise indicated, respondents could choose only one answer for a given question.

Respondents were able to add unique (volunteered) responses to certain questions, which created some difficulty in summing the percentages on those questions, as certain unique answers may have more appropriately belonged with the provided answers, or when multiple unique responses were very similar to each other. Volunteered responses are marked with an asterisk [*].

Several survey questions provided space to give comments. Those comments are provided in Appendix A.

SURVEY QUESTIONS and SUMMARY OF RESPONSES

(Unless otherwise noted, results are listed according to frequency of response.)

Q1. **Is the respondent a child or a parent?** *(60 responses)*

  71.7% Child
  28.3% Parent

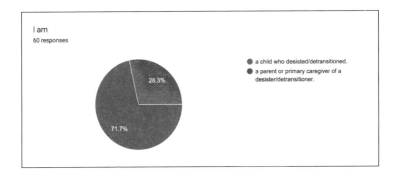

Q2. What was the child's sex at birth? *(60 responses)*

20%   *Male*

78.3%   *Female*

0.7%   *Prefer not to say*

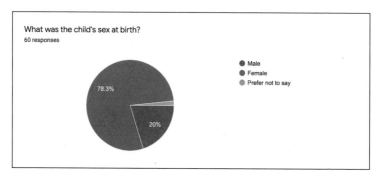

Q3. At what age did the child announce a transgender identity? *(60 responses)*

5%   *Ages 0–9*

8.3%   *Ages 10–12*

31.7%   *Ages 13–15*

26.7%   *Ages 16–18*

8.3%   *Ages 19–21*

5%   *Ages 22–25*

15%   *Ages 26+*

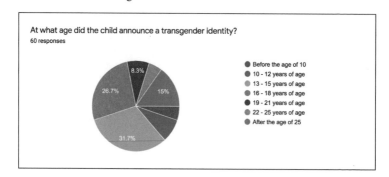

Q4. **In which of the following types of transition did the child participate?** *(60 responses. Respondents could select multiple answers.)*

81.7%	*Changed hairstyle*
78.3%	*Made use of a binder, packer, etc., in order to pass as the opposite sex*
76.7%	*Requested that a different name be used*
75%	*Changed clothing style*
73.3%	*Requested that different pronouns be used*
48.3%	*Took cross-sex hormones*
31.7%	*Changed hair color*
25%	*Underwent some form of sex-characteristic surgical alteration*
10%	*Sought some form of sex-characteristic surgical alteration, but was unable to obtain*
5%	*Took puberty blockers*
1.7%	*Legally changed name*

[No pie chart is available for Question 4.]

Q5. **If the child used puberty blockers, for how long were the puberty blockers taken?** *(4 responses)*

    50%   Longer than 2 years

    50%   1–2 years

    (Note: Question 5 offered the possible extraneous response "12 months–1 year," which is redundant with either the "6–12 months" or "1–2 years" responses. In the above percentages the single "12 months–1 year" response is grouped with the single "1–2 years" response.)

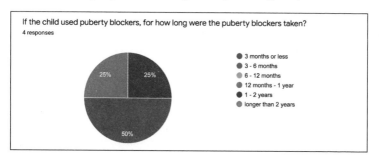

Q6. **If the child used wrong-sex hormones, for how long were the hormones taken?** *(29 responses)*

    6.9%   3 months or less

    0.0%   3–6 months

    13.8%   6–12 months

    17.2%   1–2 years

    62.1%   Longer than 2 years

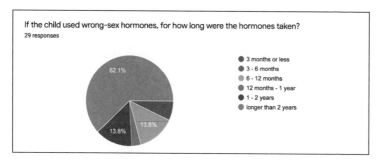

Q7. **If the child was unable to obtain a desired surgery, what was the reason?** *(17 responses)*

52.9%	*Could not finance the surgery*
29.4%	*Was prevented by a parent or caregiver*
17.6%	*Other*
0.0%	*Had health complications that prevented the surgery*
0.0%	*Was prevented by a health professional*

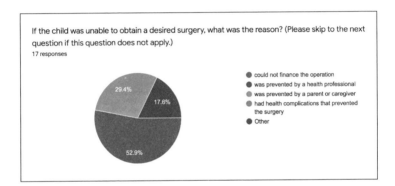

If the child was unable to obtain a desired surgery, what was the reason? (Please skip to the next question if this question does not apply.)
17 responses

- could not finance the operation
- was prevented by a health professional
- was prevented by a parent or caregiver
- had health complications that prevented the surgery
- Other

29.4%
17.6%
52.9%

Q8. **For approximately how long was the child transitioned (presenting with an alternate sex identity) in any way (socially or medically)?** *(60 responses)*

10%	*Less than 6 months*
10%	*6 months–1 year*
23.3%	*1–2 years*
30%	*3–5 years*
20%	*6–8 years*
6.7%	*More than 8 years*

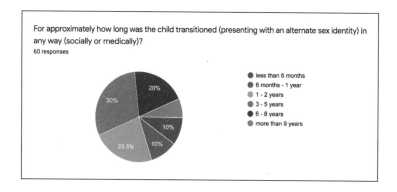

For approximately how long was the child transitioned (presenting with an alternate sex identity) in any way (socially or medically)?
60 responses

- less than 6 months
- 6 months - 1 year
- 1 - 2 years
- 3 - 5 years
- 6 - 8 years
- more than 9 years

Q9. **Where was the child first introduced to gender ideology (the concept that gender is on a continuum between maleness and femaleness, and/or that people can have the mind/brain/soul of one sex and the body of another)?**
(60 responses. Respondents could select multiple answers.)

35%	*Social media*
16.7%	*High school*
11.7%	*Middle school*
10%	*Unknown*
8.3%	*Elementary school (or earlier school)*
6.7%	*Friends*
1.7%	*College (or post-high school ed)*
1.7%	*Nooks**
1.7%	*Friend, then health class**
1.7%	*Both friends and social media**
1.7%	*Internet**
1.7%	*Anime convention**
1.7%	*Friend and high school**
0.0%	*Healthcare professional*

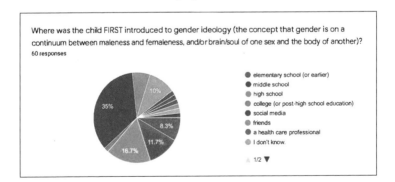

Where was the child FIRST introduced to gender ideology (the concept that gender is on a continuum between maleness and femaleness, and/or brain/soul of one sex and the body of another)?
60 responses

- elementary school (or earlier)
- middle school
- high school
- college (or post-high school education)
- social media
- friends
- a health care professional
- I don't know.

1/2 ▼

Q10. **In which communities was the child actively encouraged and affirmed in a transgender identity?** *(60 responses. Respondents could select multiple answers.)*

85%   *Social media groups*

76.7%   *Friend groups*

43.3%   *School*

28.3%   *Extended family*

25%   *Community groups (sports, activities, etc.)*

21.7%   *Job/work*

20%   *Nuclear family (parents, siblings)*

[No pie chart is available for Question 10.]

Q11. **Did the parent affirm the child in a transgender identity?** *(60 responses)*

58.3%   *No*

23.3%   *Yes*

18.3%   *Did not fully affirm, but used preferred name and pronouns*

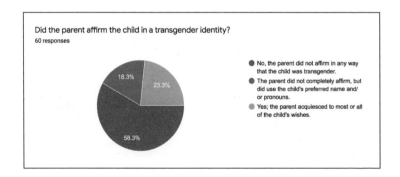

Did the parent affirm the child in a transgender identity?
60 responses

- No, the parent did not affirm in any way that the child was transgender.
- The parent did not completely affirm, but did use the child's preferred name and/or pronouns.
- Yes; the parent acquiesced to most or all of the child's wishes.

Q12. **Did the other parent affirm the child in a transgender identity?** *(60 responses)*

> *58.3% No*
>
> *21.7%*   *Did not fully affirm, but used preferred name and pronouns*
>
> *10%*   *Yes*
>
> *10%*   *The child does not have a relationship with the other parent*

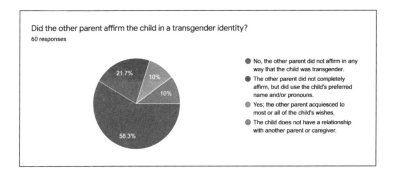

Q13. **Which of the following did the parent do after the child announced a transgender identity?** *(60 responses. Respondents could select multiple answers.)*

> *48.3%*   *Did nothing different*
>
> *36.7%*   *Arranged for outpatient therapy/counseling*
>
> *13.3%*   *Took away Internet/social media*
>
> *10%*   *Arranged for inpatient (residential) therapy/ counseling*
>
> *8.3%*   *Pulled the child and began homeschooling*
>
> *5%*   *Sent the child to live with a relative*
>
> *1.7%*   *Moved the child to a different school*
>
> *1.7%*   *Got more involved with church**

1.7% *Kicked the child out of the home**

1.7% *Completely disowned the child**

1.7% *Tried to talk the child out of the trans-ID**

1.7% *Threw away child's clothes and forced her to dress femininely; denied same-sex attraction**

[No pie chart is available for Question 13.]

Q14. If the child saw a counselor or therapist, did the counselor or therapist affirm the transgender identity?

(51 responses)

52.9% *Yes*

29.4% *No*

17.7% *Various volunteered responses (presented below exactly as entered in survey):*

"Never said yes nor said no, we studied the situation to understand, not exactly to affirm something."

"Not at first but let me believe she did after a year."

"Private counsellor didn't ... mental health team did."

"Many were seen with mixed outcomes."

"I was transitioning in the early- mid-2000s before the affirming model [had] taken over, but in the end I was affirmed."

"Reluctantly, yes."

"The first psychologist affirmed but we quickly moved her to a psychoanalyst who did not affirm."

"The first psychologist affirmed, the second one probed deeper and took longer to agree adult child was transgender."

"The therapist my mom set me up with and I did not talk about my trans identity. I later sought

therapy as an adult, where the therapist was affirm-ing of my transition."

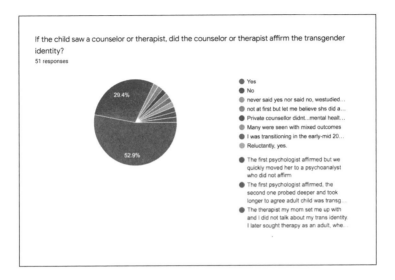

Q15 . Was the child comfortable with the counselor or therapist? *(48 (48 responses)*

> 47.9%   *Yes*
> 35.4%   *Somewhat*
> 16.7%   *No*

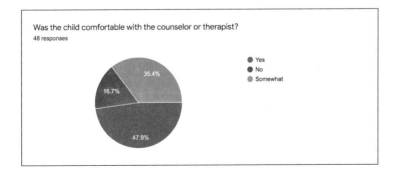

Q16. Was the parent comfortable with the counselor or therapist? *(45 responses)*

   31.1%   *Yes*
   28.9%   *Somewhat*
   26.7%   *Parent was not involved*
   13.3%   *No*

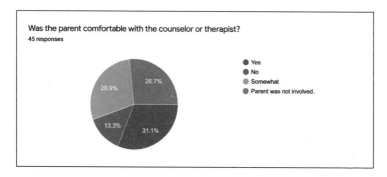

Was the parent comfortable with the counselor or therapist?
45 responses

● Yes
● No
● Somewhat
● Parent was not involved.

Q17. What were the reasons the child desisted/ detransitioned, to the best of your knowledge? *(60 responses. Respondents could select multiple answers.)*

   63.3%   *Found that transition negatively affected some aspect of life*
   58.3%   *Found that transition did not help the gender dysphoria*
   31.7%   *Was convinced by social media (illogical and/or not transgender)*
   25%   *Became bored with transgender ideology*
   23.3%   *Was convinced by parents' (or others') arguments*
   6.7%   *Was convinced by a faith leader (illogical and/or not transgender)*
   5%   *Friends desisted/detransitioned*
   5%   *Was convinced at school*
   1.7%   *Couldn't pass**

1.7%   *Dug through internal misogyny**

1.7%   *Realized the consequences**

1.7%   *Stopped feeling dysphoric**

1.7%   *Lack of support for transgender ideology in daily life**

1.7%   *A member of the opposite sex liked the child**

1.7%   *Radical feminism and self-love**

1.7%   *Found the trans community toxic and abusive**

1.7%   *Dealt with traumatic experience**

1.7%   *Realized that the trans community was controlling**

1.7%   *Investigated brain study claims and found them false**

1.7%   *Accepted self and homosexuality**

1.7%   *Diagnosed with autism**

1.7%   *Found a friend group at college**

[No pie chart is available for Question 17.]

Q18.   After the child desisted/detransitioned, did he or she immediately revert to presenting (clothing choices, hairstyle, etc.) the way he or she did prior to announcing a transgender identity? *(60 responses)*

46.7%   *No*

28.3%   *Yes*

25%   *Changed, but not to prior presentation style*

After the child desisted/detransitioned, did s/he immediately revert to presenting (clothing choices, hairstyle, etc.) the way s/he did prior to announcing a transgender identity?
60 responses

● Yes, the child immediately (or very soon after) presented physically as s/he previously did.
● No, the child continued to present physically in the same way as s/he had since announcing a transgender identity.
● The child changed his/her physical presentation immediately (or very soon after), but did not revert to his/her same prior style.

(Results for Questions 19–21 are ordered according to relational closeness from Very Good through Very Poor. A chart listing each respondent's results for Questions 19–21 follows the question summaries.)

Q19. **How was the child's relationship with his or her parent(s) prior to being introduced to gender ideology?**
(60 responses)

23.3%	*Very Good/Very Close*
30%	*Good/Somewhat Close*
20%	*Fair/Neither Close nor Strained*
15%	*Poor/Somewhat Strained*
11.7%	*Very Poor/Extremely Strained or Estranged*

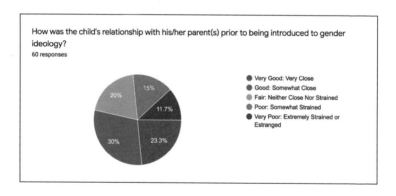

How was the child's relationship with his/her parent(s) prior to being introduced to gender ideology?
60 responses

● Very Good: Very Close
● Good: Somewhat Close
● Fair: Neither Close Nor Strained
● Poor: Somewhat Strained
● Very Poor: Extremely Strained or Estranged

Q20. **How was the child's relationship with his or her parent(s) during the period that the child was transgender-identified?** *(60 responses)*

3.3%	*Very Good/Very Close*
11.7%	*Good/Somewhat Close*
21.7%	*Fair/Neither Close nor Strained*
40%	*Poor/Somewhat Strained*
23.3%	*Very Poor/Extremely Strained or Estranged*

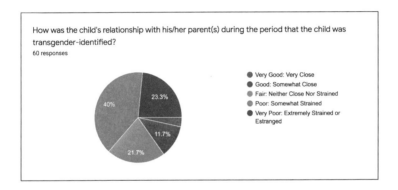

Q21. **How has the child's relationship with his or her parent(s) been since desisting/detransitioning?** *(60 responses)*

30%	*Very Good/Very Close*
26.7%	*Good/Somewhat Close*
20%	*Fair/Neither Close nor Strained*
11.7%	*Poor/Somewhat Strained*
11.7%	*Very Poor/Extremely Strained or Estranged*

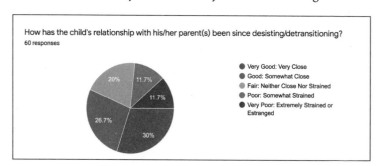

Q22. **Does the child have any diagnosed or suspected health, psychological, or neurological issues?** *(60 responses. Respondents could select multiple answers.)*

75.9%	*Depression*
50%	*Suicidal ideation*
46.6%	*Trauma*
37.9%	*Autism*
22.4%	*Suicide attempt*
13.8%	*Emotional disability*
8.6%	*Mental disability*
6.9%	*Physical disability*
3.4%	*Obsessive-compulsive disorder**
3.4%	*Anxiety**
3.4%	*Social anxiety**

    1.7%   *Other anxiety**

    1.7%   *Attention-deficit/hyperactivity disorder**

    1.7%   *Self-harm; eating disorder; poor self-image**

    1.7%   *Mood disorder**

    [No pie chart is available for Question 22.]

Q23. **To what degree does the child regret having attempted to transition sexes (to the best of your knowledge)?** *(60 responses)*

    35.6%   *Slightly regrets*

    32.2%   *Significantly regrets*

    20.3%   *Has extreme regret*

    11.9%   *Does not regret*

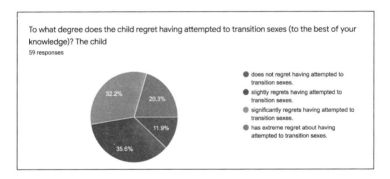

To what degree does the child regret having attempted to transition sexes (to the best of your knowledge)? The child
59 responses

- does not regret having attempted to transition sexes.
- slightly regrets having attempted to transition sexes.
- significantly regrets having attempted to transition sexes.
- has extreme regret about having attempted to transition sexes.

The following chart captures all data from Questions 19–21, which surveyed respondents' perceptions regarding the strength of the family relationship prior to, during, and following the child's attempted gender transition.

The numeric values listed in the chart correspond to the respondents' perception of familial closeness:

    Very Good/Very Close = 5

    Good/Somewhat Close = 4

    Fair/Neither Close nor Strained = 3

Poor/Somewhat Strained = 2

Very Poor/Extremely Strained or Estranged = 1

The chart is organized in descending order, with the highest "Relationship Prior to Attempted Transition" responses at the top. The letter "D" next to the Respondent # indicates that the response came from a desister/detransitioner; the letter "P" indicates that the response came from the parent of a desister/detransitioner.

Respondent #	Relationship Prior to Attempted Transition	Relationship during Attempted Transition	Relationship after Desistance/ Detransition
30 P	5	5	5
54 D	5	5	5
53 D	5	4	5
33 D	5	2	5
42 P	5	2	5
46 P	5	2	5
15 P	5	1	5
28 P	5	1	5
31 P	5	1	5
56 D	5	1	5
18 D	5	3	4
22 D	5	2	4
38 P	5	2	3
35 D	5	1	1
39 D	4	3	5
13 P	4	2	5
24 P	4	2	5
29 D	4	2	5
7 D	4	4	4

Respondent #	Relationship Prior to Attempted Transition	Relationship during Attempted Transition	Relationship after Desistance/ Detransition
19 D	4	4	4
41 D	4	4	4
43 D	4	4	4
48 D	4	4	4
1 P	4	3	4
2 D	4	3	4
32 P	4	3	4
3 D	4	2	4
11 D	4	4	3
25 P	4	1	2
52 D	4	1	2
9 D	4	2	1
59 P	4	2	1
8 D	3	3	5
34 P	3	3	5
58 D	3	3	4
14 D	3	2	4
44 D	3	2	4
17 D	3	3	3
26 D	3	3	3
4 D	3	2	3
51 P	3	2	3
50 P	3	1	3
45 D	3	1	2
49 P	3	2	1
36 D	2	2	5
23 D	2	3	4
5 D	2	2	4

Respondent #	Relationship Prior to Attempted Transition	Relationship during Attempted Transition	Relationship after Desistance/ Detransition
37 D	2	3	3
57 D	2	2	3
60 D	2	2	3
40 D	2	1	3
10 D	2	2	2
16 D	2	2	2
20 D	1	3	5
6 D	1	2	3
55 D	1	2	2
27 D	1	1	2
12 D	1	1	1
21 D	1	1	1
47 D	1	1	1

It is compelling to note that in the majority of cases, the strength/ closeness of the familial relationship dropped during the child's attempted gender transition, but typically rose again to the same or greater level of closeness following desistance/detransition. In only four cases was the strength of the family relationship perceived to fall after desistance/detransition. It is also interesting to note that all results indicating the strength of the familial relationship prior to attempted transition as Poor (2) or Very Poor (1) came from desisters/detransitioners, rather than from parents.

However, a number of caveats to the interpretation of the above data must be kept in mind:

✠ The survey subjects were not randomly selected from among the population of all detransitioners; respondents self-selected to take this survey.

✠ Surveys always reflect personal perception and bias, which may significantly deviate from others' perceptions and biases, and from reality. Personal perceptions may also be a function of the respondent's frame of mind at the particular moment the survey was taken, as opposed to reflecting a more longitudinal or general state of perception. If, for example, the respondent recently had an argument with his or her parent, that event may inspire a lower relationship-strength score than would be registered at a different moment in time.

✠ Demographic information, such as respondents' current age, health status, personal history, and family makeup, is not reflected in the above table.

✠ It is unknown how many results include pairs of desister/ detransitioner and parent/primary caregiver relationships. It would be interesting to compare perceptions of family relationships by both a desister/detransitioner and his or her parent(s), but that is beyond the scope of data collected by this survey.

✠ Because the survey could be taken anonymously, and no authentication of results occurred beyond removing those that were obviously invalid (as described in the beginning of this appendix), it is possible that fabricated/false information was provided to the survey.

Again, perhaps the most important result that can be taken away from this survey is the necessity and value of more comprehensive and detailed research into the phenomenon of desistance/detransition. Any serious inquirer recognizes there is an alarming paucity of research in this area. Open surveys such as this one are how a body of knowledge begins to develop. It is our hope that this data will help inform and guide future projects with larger numbers of subjects over longer periods of time.

Universal Opt-Out Letter for Sexuality and Gender Ideology Training at School

IF FOR SOME REASON you cannot pull your child from a school that may not respect parental authority over children's safety and education, you can try to protect your child from exposure to controversial and/or flawed sexuality and gender ideology information by informing the school of your expectations. The letter below may be sent to teachers, principals, administrators, and/or school board members to instruct them regarding what may or may not be presented to your children. The letter may be used verbatim (please fill in school district and personal information as necessary) or may be edited to meet your child's and family's specific needs.

No guarantees exist, however, that your school or any particular employee within your school will respect your instructions. Policies around transgender-identified students are codifying schools' willingness to be deceptive to parents and guardians. Please be aware that disregard for such instructions is quite possible.

DATE

PARENTS' ADDRESS
PARENTS' ADDRESS
PARENTS' ADDRESS

TEACHER'S/PRINCIPAL'S NAME
NAME OF SCHOOL DISTRICT

Dear NAME,

My child, CHILD'S NAME, is to be opted out of all Family Life Education curriculum for school year 20XX-XX. Further, CHILD'S NAME is not to be included in any lessons, activities, or discussions in any class, club, or activity led by teachers, staff, administrators, or guest speakers, or other students around the following topics:

Human Sexuality
Sexual Orientation
Transgender Issues
Family Composition
Gender Identity

If any part of a unit of curriculum contains references to any of the above topics, please provide CHILD'S NAME with an alternative curriculum package or relevant material for that subject which does not reference the above topics. The only exception to this opt-out will be curriculum regarding the biological processes of reproduction for humans and/or animals in a science class or unit.

Our family does not give consent for NAME OF SCHOOL to provide any instruction to CHILD'S NAME on any of the above topics. These topics will be treated at home, by CHILD'S NAME parents/guardians.

Furthermore, no information about anything that takes place at school regarding CHILD'S NAME is to be withheld from us, his/her parents/legal guardians, even should our child request it. According to the Family Educational Rights and Privacy Act, "Parents or eligible students have the right to inspect and review the student's education records maintained by the school." We do not consider any record kept by any school staff member to be exempt from this directive.

If you have any questions about these instructions, please do not hesitate to inquire.

SIGNATURE
NAME
CONTACT INFORMATION

Resources

Advocates Protecting Children
www.advocatesprotectingchildren.org

Arlington Parent Coalition
https://www.arlingtonparentcoa.wixsite.com/arlingtonparentcoa

Gender Dysphoria Support Network
https://genderdysphoriasupportnetwork.com/

Inspired Teen Therapy (Sasha Ayad, M. Ed., LPC)
https://inspiredteentherapy.com/

*Irreversible Damage: The Transgender Craze
Seducing Our Daughters*
Abigail Shrier

Parent Resource Guide (Minnesota Family Council)
https://www.mfc.org/request-the-parent-resource-guide

Parents of ROGD Kids (Support Group Network)
https://www.parentsofrogdkids.com/

Rethink Identity Medicine Ethics, Inc.
https://www.rethinkime.org/

Society for Evidence-Based Gender Medicine
https://www.segm.org/

Transgender Trend (Questioning the Trans Narrative)
https://www.transgendertrend.com/

Understanding Transgender Issues (Family Watch International)
https://www.familywatch.org/transgenderissues/

When Harry Became Sally: Responding to the Transgender Moment
Ryan T. Anderson

Glossary

The following terms are defined as the author under-stands their use, but not necessarily as LGB and TQ organizations would claim they are defined. Definitions are pulled from LGB and TQ materials, dictionaries, and/or the personal experience of the author.

Ally: a person who supports all LGB and TQ issues and ideologies. This is becoming more and more subjective, as many transgender-rights activists argue that homosexuals are transphobic if they refuse to date transgender-identified people who claim to be their preferred sex partners.

Androgynous: of indeterminate sex; having characteristics of both maleness and femaleness.

Antagonists: as used in this book, people who are leading your child deeper into the gender cult.

Asexual: lacking any sexual attractions to others.

Biological sex: the sex that one was born, male or female, as evidenced by chromosomes, external anatomy (genitals, breasts), and internal anatomy (sex glands and organs).

Biphobia: prejudice against bisexual people. In current vernacular this term is applied to anyone who disagrees with anything that a bisexual person says, wants, or believes.

Bisexual: experiencing sexual attraction to both males and females.

Cis-: a prefix indicating that one's behavior or preferences align with typical or biological expectations (cisgender, cis-sexual, cis-man, etc.). This is a pejorative and nonsensical term, since no one feels completely comfortable with his or her body at all times.

Cisgender: a person whose gender identity aligns with his or her birth sex. Near antonym to **Queer.**

Closeted: an LGB/TQ person who hides his or her sexuality and/ or gender identity from most other people. Antonym of **Living Openly.**

Coming out: used as a verb or a noun, "coming out" means announcing one's sexuality or gender identity publicly.

Deadname: the name parents gave to a child when he or she was born, which is rejected in favor of a self-chosen transgender name.

Desister: a person who believed him- or herself to be transgender but has since accepted his or her birth sex as reality.

Detransitioner: a person who presented as other than his or her birth sex, transitioning socially and/or medically, but has since accepted his or her birth sex as reality and presents as such.

Fantasy defense: a sexual predator's claim that he did not intend to carry out sexual activities but was merely indulging in harmless fantasy, and/or that the victim misconstrued fantasy for reality: "It never actually happened."[150]

FTM: female to male transgender. Opposite of **MTF.**

Gay: homosexual, or attracted to members of one's own sex. Usually applied to males, but not exclusively.

Gender clinic: a center that engages in experimental medical interventions where nearly every client is deemed appropriate for sex transition and assisted in attempted social and medical transition to a different sex.

Gender dysphoria: a diagnostic term describing when one's sense of his or her gender identity does not always and/or fully match his or her biological sex.

Gender-expansive: a term related to the ideology that gender is on a spectrum, and that one can be located anywhere on that spectrum.

Gender expression: one's external presentation of one's gender identity; dressing and behaving like a particular sex or combination of the sexes, based on stereotypes.

Gender-fluid: not subscribing to one fixed gender; one whose sense of gender identity changes all the time.

Gender identity: a nonsensical term referring to one's self-perception as male, female, or something in between; based entirely on stereotypes.

Gender-nonconforming: not aligning with stereotypes of one's biological sex.

Genderqueer: someone who embraces gender fluidity, who doesn't present according to biological sex stereotypes. Near synonym to **Nonbinary.**

Gender transition: attempting to change sexes (or gender expression) or to impersonate another sex (or gender expression) via social transition (dressing according to stereotypes of a different sex) or medical transition (taking puberty blockers and/or cross-sex hormones, and/or having surgeries). Gender transition is an attempt to make the body align with the mind.

Glitter families: older transgender-identified people who groom children to reject their families of origin and consider the transgender-identified adults their new families.

GLSEN: Gay, Lesbian, and Straight Education Network; organization creating and disseminating homosexuality and transgenderism propaganda, policy, and curricula.

Grooming: specific strategies used by child predators to gain access to children for their sexual exploitation.[151]

Homophobia: fear or hatred of people who are same-sex attracted.

Homosexual: attracted to people of the same sex as oneself. Synonym to **Gay** and **Same-sex attracted**.

HRC: The Human Rights Campaign Foundation; the funding and lobby organization for the homosexual and transgender communities.

Intersex: in popular, current usage, a person who was born with mixed anatomical features of maleness and femaleness. In one recent study, the sex of a newborn was not clear from inspection of genitalia in about one in one thousand births.[152] These babies have *disorders of sexual development*. Chromosomes and internal organs can be evaluated to clarify a child's sex. Some disorders of sexual development might not be discovered until puberty or after.

Lesbian: a woman who is sexually attracted to other women.

LGBTQ: An acronym for Lesbian, Gay, Bisexual, Transgender, and Queer.

LGB and TQ: An acronym for Lesbian, Gay, and Bisexual; Transgender and Queer, which delineates the very different populations of LGB people and TQ people.

Living openly: describes those who do not hide their sexuality and/or gender identities. Antonym of **Closeted.**

Misgendering: calling someone by a pronoun they do not prefer (i.e., the biologically and grammatically correct pronoun or title).

MTF: Male to female transgender. Opposite of **FTM.**

Nonbinary: Someone who does not view himself or herself as aligning with either maleness or femaleness. Near synonym to **Genderqueer.**

Outing: (verb) revealing another person's sexuality and/or gender identity without permission to do so.

Pansexual: sexually attracted to anyone at any time; willing to be sexual partners with anyone.

Peak: (verb) recognizing that gender ideology is unsound; becoming gender-critical.

Pedophile: an adult who is sexually attracted to prepubescent children. Pedophilia is still considered a mental disorder.

Polyamory: multiple (more than two) sexual partners in relationship with each other at one time.

Presentation (or Present [v]): how one shows him- or herself to the world; the clothing, hairstyle, and mannerism choices that reflect one's gender (sex) status, based on cultural stereotypes.

Pronouns (also Preferred pronouns): the grammatical reference used in place of a proper noun. Transgender persons demand to be referred to by different pronouns than would be linguistically accurate (e.g., a man tells you that his pronouns are "she/her").

Protagonists: as used in this book, people who are working with you to help pull your child out of the gender cult.

Queer: an umbrella term to express any sexual and/or gender orientation/presentation other than being a **Cisgender** heterosexual. Near antonym to **Cisgender**.

Questioning: describes someone who is exploring his or her sexuality and/or gender.

Safe person/space: indicates a person, place, or group that will affirm the child in transition and medicalization, and is willing to deceive/undermine parents toward that goal.

Same-sex attracted: attracted to people of the same sex as oneself. Synonym to **Homosexual**. Near synonym to **Gay** (males) and **Lesbian** (females).

Sex assigned at birth: one's biological sex. This term has been created to propagate the false idea that there is no such thing as biological sex, only the gender that someone (a doctor or parent) "assigned" to a child based on the child's genitalia.

Sexual orientation: the nature of one's sexual and/or romantic attractions. LGB/TQ organizations often claim that sexual orientation is inherent and immutable, but this assertion is belied by the number of people who "come out" as homosexual in middle age or beyond, and those who become or return to being heterosexual after counseling and/or therapy.[153]

Stereotype: a widely held idea or image of a person, which is fixed and oversimplified: e.g., "all girls like pink," "all boys like sports," "women can't do math."

Supportive: willing to capitulate to all demands of the transgender-identified person.

TERF: Trans-Exclusive Radical Feminist; originally referred to radical feminists who did not accept transgender ideology, but is currently used as a slur against anyone who does not fully capitulate to transgender activist's agenda.

Transgender: claiming to feel a mismatch between one's biological sex and one's sense of self; presenting oneself to the world according to stereotypes that do not align with those of one's biological (birth) sex.

Transphobia: fear or hatred of people who are transgender. In current vernacular this term is applied to anyone who disagrees with anything that a transgender person says, wants, or believes.

Unsupportive: unwilling to capitulate to all demands of the transgender-identified person.

About the Author

Maria Keffler is a cofounder of Advocates Protecting Children, which serves and supports churches, schools, organizations, families, and individuals who seek facts and guidance on responding to gender ideology and activism. Ms. Keffler also is a cofounder of the Arlington Parent Coalition, a watchdog group in Arlington, Virginia, that works to safeguard parents' rights and children's safety in public education. An author, speaker, and teacher with a background in educational psychology, Ms. Keffler has fought to protect children from unethical activism and dangerous policies around sexuality and transgender ideology since 2018. She and her husband have three young adult and teenage children.

Endnotes

The author does not endorse the opinions or perspectives of any individuals or organizations represented in the resources below. Be aware that certain citation sources may have views on topics in this book which conflict with the author's.

1   Maria Keffler and Erin Brewer, *Commonsense Care*, Partners for Ethical Care, YouTube video series, December 24, 2020–October 14, 2021, https://www.youtube.com/playlist?list=PLPM5Sjop1VBspuUwXd4tgkg1UOPVDKzZi.

2   "The Surge in Referral Rates of Girls to the Tavistock Continues to Rise," Transgender Trend, July 1, 2019, https://www.transgendertrend.com/surge-referral-rates-girls-tavistock-continues-rise/.

3   Kendra Cherry, "Understanding Erikson's Stages of Development," Verywell Mind, updated May 2, 2024, from https://www.verywellmind.com/erik-eriksons-stages-of-psychosocial-development-2795740.

4   "John Money (1921–2006)," GoodTherapy, updated July 8, 2015, https://www.goodtherapy.org/famous-psychologists/john-money.html.

5   John Colapinto, *As Nature Made Him: The Boy Who Was Raised as a Girl* (New York: Harper Collins, 2000).

6   Phil Gaetano, "David Reimer and John Money Gender Reassignment Controversy: The John/Joan Case," Embryo Project Encyclopedia, November 15, 2017, https://embryo.asu.edu/pages/david-reimer-and-john-money-gender-reassignment-controversy-johnjoan-case.

7   Sandra G. Boodman, "A Terrible Accident, a Dismal Failure," *Washington Post*, February 29, 2000, https://www.washingtonpost.com/archive/lifestyle/wellness/2000/02/29/a-terrible-accident-a-dismal-failure/83850bc4-b27a-417e-ba85-3693a4cafdd0/.

8   Meagan Day, "How One of America's Best Medical Schools Started a Secret Transgender Surgery Clinic," Medium, November 15, 2016. https://medium. com/timeline/americas-first-transgender-clinic-b56928e20f5f; Linell Smith, "A Bright New Start for Transgender Health," Johns Hopkins Medicine, November 28, 2018, https://www.hopkinsmedicine.org/news/articles/ gender-affirming-treatment.

9   Sasha Ayad, in *Dysphoric: A Four-Part Documentary Series*, part 1, Lime Soda Films, January 29, 2021, at 7:28–8:05, https://youtu.be/w8taOdnXD6o.

10 Carissa R. Violante, "Every Cell has a Sex: X and Y and the Future of Health Care," Yale School of Medicine, August 30, 2016, https://medicine.yale.edu/ news-article/13321/.

11 "Cult" (British), Dictionary.com, accessed June 21, 2024, https://www. dictionary.com/browse/cult.

12 Alex Newman, "Teacher Recruits 'Most Emotionally Unstable' Kids for LGBT Club," New American, August 15, 2000. https://thenewamerican. com/teacher-recruits-most-emotionally-unstable-kids-for-lgbt-club/.

13 Maria Keffler, "Horrified Mother Gets Front Row Seat to Sex and Gender Indoctrination Strategy Meeting," Partners for Ethical Care, February 8, 2021, https://www.partnersforethicalcare.com/post/horrified-mother-gets-front-row-seat-to-sex-gender-indoctrination-strategy-meeting.

14 Rachel Goldberg, "I Was Recruited by Allison Mack's Sex Cult," Vulture, May 14, 2018, https://www.vulture.com/2018/05/i-was-recruited-for-allison-macks-sex-cult.html.

15 "The APS Modus Operandi: Ask Us No Questions, We'll Tell You No Lies," Arlington Parent Coalition. February 7, 2020. https:// arlingtonparentcoa.wixsite.com/arlingtonparentcoa/post/ the-aps-modus-operandi-ask-us-no-questions-we-ll-tell-you-no-lies.

16 Abigail Shrier, *Irreversible Damage: The Transgender Craze Seducing Our Daughters* (Washington, DC: Regnery, 2000), 41–57.

17 Terrance Heath, "Here's Your Complete List of LGBTQ Holidays and Commemorations," LGBTQ Nation, updated October 17, 2020, https://www.lgbtqnation.com/2018/10/ heres-complete-list-lgbtq-holidays-commemorations-just-time-spirit-day/.

18 Maria Keffler, "Transgender Religion Codified and Enforced at School," Partners for Ethical Care, December 23, 2020, https://www.partnersforethicalcare.com/post/transgender-religion-codified-enforced-at-school.

19 Mark D. Griffiths, "Love Bombing: What Is It and Is It Addictive?" February 14, 2019, Psychology Today, https://www.psychologytoday.com/us/blog/ in-excess/201902/love-bombing.

20 Sarah R., "I Hated Her Guts at the Time: A Trans-Desister and Her Mom Tell Their Story," 4th Wave Now, January 18, 2018, https://4thwavenow.com/tag/ ladyantitheist/.

21 Casey Bond, "How MLMs and Cults Use the Same Mind Control Techniques," Huff Post, updated January 8, 2021, https://www.huffpost.com/entry/multilevel-marketing-companies-mlms-cults-similarities_l_5d49f8c2e4b09e72973df3d3.

22 "GLSEN Safe Space Kit: Be an ALLY to LGBTQ Youth!" GLSEN, accessed August 19, 2020, https://www.glsen.org/activity/glsen-safe-space-kit-be-ally-lgbtq-youth.

23 Trans-Exclusive Radical Feminist. The slur has come to be applied to any woman who questions the transgender narrative in any way.

24 "Problems with a Politicized Climate of Harassment and Censorship," Gender Health Query, June 1, 2019, https://www.genderhq.org/trans-activism-identity-politics-harassment-censorship.

25 Fr. Dwight Longenecker, "4 Danger Signs of Cult-Like Behavior, and 4 Antidotes," April 24, 2017, https://www.ncregister.com/blog/4-danger-signs-of-cult-like-behavior-and-4-antidotes.

26 "MtoF Tells Trans Kids to Dump Moms on Mother's Day and Join the "Glitter-Queer" Family of Adult Trans Activists," 4th Wave Now, May 14, 2017, https://4thwavenow.com/2017/05/14/mtof-tells-trans-kids-to-dump-moms-on-mothers-day-and-join-the-glitter-queer-family-of-adult-trans-activists/.

27 Tré Goins-Phillips, "Judge Bars Wisconsin School District from Hiding Students' Gender Identities from Parents," Faithwire, September 30, 2020, https://www.faithwire.com/2020/09/30/judge-bars-wisconsin-school-district-from-hiding-students-gender-identities-from-parents/.

28 Matt Davis, "4 Psychological Techniques Cults Use to Recruit Members," Big Think, updated February 27, 2023, https://bigthink.com/culture-religion/four-cult-recruitment-techniques?rebelltitem=5#rebelltitem5.

29 Melissa Dittmann, "Cults of Hatred," *Monitor on Psychology* 33, no. 10 (November 2002): 30, https://www.apa.org/monitor/nov02/cults.

30 "Glossary of Terms," Human Rights Campaign. updated May 31, 2023, https://www.hrc.org/resources/glossary-of-terms.

31 "Yes, They Taught Your Kids This," Arlington Parent Coalition, May 26, 2019, May 27). https://arlingtonparentcoa.wixsite.com/arlingtonparentcoa/post/yes-they-taught-your-kids-this.

32 Charity Norman, "Eight Steps to Mind Control: How Cults Suck Ordinary People In," *New Zealand Herald*, May 26, 2017, https://www.nzherald.co.nz/lifestyle/eight-steps-to-mind-control-how-cults-suck-ordinary-people-in/JVANMWX7XTTXBC2AS2C3GN3SX4/.

33 Mary Rice Hasson, " 'It Isn't Hate to Speak the Truth': J. K. Rowling Takes a Stand against Gender Ideology, and We Should Stand with Her," *Our Sunday Visitor*, June 15, 2020, https://www.osvnews.com/2020/06/15/

it-isnt-hate-to-speak-the-truth-j-k-rowling-takes-a-stand-against-gender-ideology-and-we-should-stand-with-her/.

34   Sam Fleischacker, "Cult vs. Religion: What's the Difference?" *Baltimore Sun*, updated June 4, 2019, https://www.baltimoresun.com/opinion/bs-xpm-2011-10-13-bs-ed-mormons-20111013-story.html.

35   Bella D., "10 Former Cult Members and Their Chilling Stories," Listverse, July 29, 2017, https://listverse.com/2017/07/29/10-former-cult-members-and-their-chilling-stories/.

36   "Preparations before Leaving for Hajj," IslamiCity, August 08, 2018. https://www.islamicity.org/5557/preparations-before-leaving-for-hajj/.

37   Emma Reynolds,"Life after Gloriavale, the Repressive Cult Run By an Australian Sex Offender," News.com.au, August 30, 2017, https://www.news.com.au/lifestyle/real-life/true-stories/life-after-gloriavale-the-repressive-cult-run-by-an-australian-sex-offender/news-story/390f38fedac3f684e80f9204b71bfef5.

38   Westboro Baptist Church website, accessed February 3, 2021, https://godhatesfags.com/.

39   Annette Kuhn et al., "Quality of Life 15 Years after Sex Reassignment Surgery for Transsexualism," *Reproductive Surgery* 92, no. 5 (November 2009): 1685–1589, https://doi.org/10.1016/j.fertnstert.2008.08.126; "MTF Vaginoplasty: What Patients Need to Know before Choosing a Technique," MTFsurgery.net, updated November 28, 2023, https://www.mtfsurgery.net/mtf-vaginoplasty.htm; Tyler O'Neil, "Detransitioners Open Up about How Transgender 'Medicine' Left Them Scarred for Life," PJ Media, March 12, 2021, https://pjmedia.com/news-and-politics/tyler-o-neil/2021/03/12/detransitioners-open-up-transgender-identity-was-a-way-to-cope-with-my-trauma-and-body-hatred-n1432065.

40   Mitch Kellaway, "Report: Trans Americans four times more likely to live in poverty," Advocate, February 18, 2015, https://www.advocate.com/politics/transgender/2015/02/18/report-trans-americans-four-times-more-likely-live-poverty; Kevin Nadal, Kristin Davidoff, and Whitney Fujii-Doe, "Transgender Women and the Sex Work Industry: Roots in Systemic, Institutional, and Interpersonal Discrimination," *Journal of Trauma and Dissociation* 15, no. 2 (2014): 169–183, https://doi.org/10.1080/15299732.2014.867572; Andre Van Mol et al., "Correction: Transgender Surgery Provides No Mental Health Benefit," Public Discourse, September 13, 2020, https://www.thepublicdiscourse.com/2020/09/71296/.

41   Cecilia Dhejne et al., "Long-Term Follow-Up of Transsexual Persons Undergoing Sex Reassignment Surgery: Cohort Study in Sweden," PLOS ONE, February 22, 2011, https://doi.org/10.1371/journal.pone.0016885.

42 Jennifer Bilek, "Who Are the Rich, White Men Institutionalizing Transgender Ideology?" The Federalist, February 20, 2018, https://thefederalist.com/2018/02/20/rich-white-men-institutionalizing-transgender-ideology/.

43 Maria Keffler, "All about the Money: Sex Reassignment Surgery Touted as 'Growth Market.'" Partners for Ethical Care, December 2, 2020, https://www.partnersforethicalcare.com/post/all-about-the-money-sex-reassignment-surgery-touted-as-growth-market.

44 Jody L. Herman et al., "Age of Individuals Who Identify as Transgender in the United States," Williams Institute, June 17, 2020, accessed February 4, 2021, https://williamsinstitute.law.ucla.edu/publications/age-trans-individuals-us/.

45 Lisa Littman, "Parent Reports of Adolescents and Young Adults Perceived to Show Signs of a Rapid Onset of Gender Dysphoria," PLOS ONE, August 16, 2018, https://journals.plos.org/plosone/article?id=10.1371%2Fjournal.pone.0202330.

46 Abigail Shrier, "Inside Planned Parenthood's Gender Business," Real Clear Politics, February 11, 2021, https://www.realclearpolitics.com/2021/02/11/inside_planned_parenthoods_gender_business_535705.html#!; Ariana Eunjung Cha, "Planned Parenthood to Open Reproductive Health Centers at 50 Los Angeles High Schools, *Washington Post*, December 11, 2019, https://www.washingtonpost.com/health/2019/12/11/planned-parenthood-open-reproductive-health-centers-los-angeles-high-schools/.

47 Erin Brewer, "Autism and Gender Identity," October 17, 2020, YouTube video, 52:24, https://youtu.be/GjXcK77XjdY.

48 Maria Keffler and Erin Brewer, "Trauma and Gender Dysphoria," Partners for Ethical Care, November 10, 2021, YouTube video, 1:03:09, https://youtu.be/D5f3XVoH1_o?si=G8vhKaoahrb5QYvj.

49 "Johanna Olson-Kennedy and the US Gender Affirmative Approach," Transgender Trend, April 17, 2019, June 19). https://www.transgendertrend.com/johanna-olson-kennedy-gender-affirmative-approach/.

50 Charlene L. Edge, "Cults and Identity Theft," Charlene L. Edge: Writer on the Wing, September 9, 2015, https://charleneedge.com/cults-identity-theft/.

51 A. Aharon, "The Secret Tactics of Glitter Moms: A Tale of Betrayal and Grooming," January 29, 2021, accessed February 6, 2021, https://www.transgenderabuse.org/post/the-secret-tactics-of-glitter-moms-a-tale-of-betrayal-and-grooming. As of June 2024, this website is no longer in operation and the article is not available elsewhere.

52 Leonard Holmes, "The Debate over Repressed and Recovered Memories," Verywell Mind, updated November 29, 2020, https://www.verywellmind.com/the-debate-over-recovered-memories-2330516.

53 Brittany Carrico, "What Is Emotional Invalidation?" updated July 19, 2021, https://www.psychcentral.com/blog/emotionally-sensitive/2012/02/reasons-you-and-others-invalidate-your-emotional-experience#1.

54 "Gender Identity: Can a 5'9 White Guy Be a 6'5 Chinese Woman?" Family Policy Institute of Washington, April 13, 2016, YouTube video, 4:13, https://youtu.be/xfO1veFs6Ho.

55 Maria Keffler and Erin Brewer, "Boundaries: Setting Them and Enforcing Them," Partners for Ethical Care, January 7, 2021, YouTube video, 36:34, https://youtu.be/W2YKagwtenc.

56 Shrier, *Irreversible Damage*.

57 "False Dichotomy — Definition and Examples," Logical Fallacy, September 9, 2020, https://www.logical-fallacy.com/articles/false-dilemma/.

58 Tina Traster, "Trans Kids May Reject Family, Not the Other Way Around," Transgender Trend, November 20, 2020, https://www.transgendertrend.com/trans-kids-reject-family-not-other-way-around/.

59 Yvonne K. Fulbright, "10 Ways to Improve Any Relationship," Psychology Today, December 30, 2014, https://www.psychologytoday.com/us/blog/mate-relate-and-communicate/201412/10-ways-improve-any-relationship.

60 "Cults in Our Midst," Cult Education Institute, accessed March 13, 2021, https://culteducation.com/group/1273-recovery/17912-cults-in-our-midst-leaving-a-cult-and-recoverings.html.

61 Jeremiah Keenan, " 'Doctor' Advises Threatening Suicide to Get Trans Treatments for Kids," April 1, 2019, https://thefederalist.com/2019/04/01/doctor-advises-threatening-suicide-get-transgender-treatments-kids/.

62 Leonard Mlodinow, "How We Communicate Through Body Language." Psychology Today, May 29, 2012, accessed July 19, 2024, https://www.psychologytoday.com/us/blog/subliminal/201205/how-we-communicate-through-body-language.

63 Kendra Cherry, "How to Understand and Identify Passive-Aggressive Behavior," Verywell Mind, updated September 16, 2022, https://www.verywellmind.com/what-is-passive-aggressive-behavior-2795481.

64 Amy Morin, "Using Praise to Encourage Good Behaviors," Verwell Family, updated April 30, 2021, https://www.verywellfamily.com/praise-build-childrens-character-1094902.

65 Itamar Shatz, "The Benjamin Franklin Effect: Build Rapport by Asking for Favors," Effectiviology, accessed June 22, 2024, https://effectiviology.com/benjamin-franklin-effect/.

66 Curt Thompson, *Anatomy of the Soul: Surprising Connections between Neuroscience and Spiritual Practices That Can Transform Your Life and Relationships* (Carol Stream, IL: Tyndale Momentum, 2010).

67 Bryan Zitzman, "Why Your Family Matters — Importance of Family," Family Today, accessed June 22, 2024, https://www.familytoday.com/relationships/importance-of-family/.

68 Marisa LaScala, "Why Do Children Have Imaginary Friends, and How Far Do You Have to Play Along?" *Good Housekeeping*, August 9, 2019,

https://www.goodhousekeeping.com/life/parenting/a28579180/
why-children-have-imaginary-friends/.

69 Michelle Cretella, "I'm a Pediatrician. Here's What I Did When a Little Boy
Patient Said He Was a Girl," Daily Signal, December 11, 2017, https://www.
dailysignal.com/2017/12/11/cretella-transcript/.

70 "Developmental Appropriateness and the Comprehensive Sex
Ed Agenda," Arlington Parent Coalition, September 22, 2019,
https://arlingtonparentcoa.wixsite.com/arlingtonparentcoa/post/
developmental-appropriateness-the-comprehensive-sex-ed-agenda.

71 Kendra Cherry, "Piaget's 4 Stages of Cognitive Development Explained,"
Verywell Mind, updated May 1, 2024, https://www.verywellmind.com/
piagets-stages-of-cognitive-development-2795457.

72 Gwen Dewar, "Praise and Intelligence: The Argument for Process-Based
Praise," Parenting Science, last modified April 2024, http://www.parenting-
science.com/praise-and-intelligence.html.

73 Jonathan Van Maren, "So It's Now Acceptable to Call Mispronouncing a
Transgender Name an Act of Violence?" LifeSiteNews, October 17, 2019,
https://www.lifesitenews.com/blogs/so-its-now-acceptable-to-call-mispro-
nouncing-a-transgender-name-an-act-of-violence.

74 Lisa Marchiano, "The Ranks of Gender etransitioners Are Growing. We
Need to Understand Why," Quillette, January 2, 2020, https://quillette.
com/2020/01/02/the-ranks-of-gender-detransitioners-are-growing-we-
need-to-understand-why/.

75 "Updated: Brown Statements on Gender Dysphoria Study," Brown University,
March 19, 2019, https://www.brown.edu/news/2019-03-19/gender.

76 Lisa Littman, "Parent Reports of Adolescents and Young Adults Perceived
to Show Signs of a Rapid Onset of Gender Dysphoria," PLOS ONE, August
16, 2018, https://journals.plos.org/plosone/article?id=10.1371%2Fjournal.
pone.0202330.

77 Maria Keffler and Erin Brewer, "Autism and GenderDysphoria," Partners for
Ethical Care, February 25, 2021, YouTube video, 59:06, https://youtu.be/
HsbkWJEuAgc.

78 Anglia Ruskin University, "Study Finds Transgender, Non-binary Autism
Link," Medical Press, July 16. 2019, https://medicalxpress.com/news/2019-
07-transgender-non-binary-autism-link.html.

79 "Autism Statistics and Facts." Autism Speaks, March 24, 2023, https://www.
autismspeaks.org/autism-statistics-asd.

80 Sian Griffiths, "Autistic Girls Seeking Answers 'Are Seizing on Sex Change,' "
Times (UK), January 9, 2021, https://www.thetimes.co.uk/article/
autistic-girls-seeking-answers-are-seizing-on-sex-change-3r82850gw.

81 Scott Barry Kaufman, "Rethinking Autism: From Social Awkwardness to Social Creativity," June 14, 2017,

Behavioral Scientiest, https://behavioralscientist.org/rethinking-autism-social-awkwardness-social-creativity/.

82   Laina Eartharcher, "Asperger's/Autism and 'Black-and-White Thinking,'"
      March 8, 2017, *The Silent Wave* (blog), https://thesilentwaveblog.wordpress.
      com/2017/03/08/aspergers-autism-and-black-and-white-thinking/.

83   "Autism and Dealing with Change," *The Autism Blog*, Seattle Chil-
      dren's, February 8, 2013, https://theautismblog.seattlechildrens.org/
      autism-and-dealing-with-change/

84   "10 Symptoms of High-Functioning Autism," Applied Behavior Analysis
      Programs Guide, accessed February 12, 2021, https://www.appliedbehavior-
      analysisprograms.com/lists/5-symptoms-of-high-functioning-autism/.

85   Erin Brewer, "Autism and Gender Identity," October 17, 2020, YouTube video,
      52:24, https://youtu.be/GjXcK77XjdY.

86   Walt Heyer, "Childhood Sexual Abuse, Gender Dysphoria, and Transition
      Regret: Billy's Story," Public Discourse, March 26, 2018, https://www.the-
      publicdiscourse.com/2018/03/21178/.

87   Erin Brewer, "I Was a Trans Kid," Eagle Forum, November 10, 2019, YouTube
      video, 23:11, https://youtu.be/GFphNvRraLA.

88   "What Are Dissociative Disorders?" American Psychiatric Association, ac-
      cessed February 13, 2021, https://www.psychiatry.org/patients-families/
      dissociative-disorders/what-are-dissociative-disorders.

89   Cecilia Dhejne et al., "Mental Health and Gender Dysphoria: A Review of
      the Literature," *International Review of Psychiatry* 28, no. 1 (2016): 44–57,
      https://www.tandfonline.com/doi/abs/10.3109/09540261.2015.1115753.

90   A. W. Geiger and Leslie Davis, "A Growing Number of American Teenag-
      ers — Particularly Girls — Are Facing Depression," Pew Research Center, July
      12, 2019, https://www.pewresearch.org/fact-tank/2019/07/12/a-growing-
      number-of-american-teenagers-particularly-girls-are-facing-depression/.

91   Walt Heyer, "Transgenders, 4 Studies Say It's Mental Disorders,"
      Walt Heyer Ministries, November 16, 2000, https://waltheyer.com/
      transgenders-4-studies-say-its-mental-disorders/.

92   Cecilia Dhejne, et al., "Long-Term Follow-Up of Transsexual Persons Under-
      going Sex Reassignment Surgery: Cohort Study in Sweden," *PLOS ONE* 6, no.
      2 (February 22, 2011), https://pubmed.ncbi.nlm.nih.gov/21364939/.

93   Ryan T. Anderson, "Sex Reassignment Doesn't Work. Here Is the Evidence,"
      Heritage Foundation, March 9, 2018, https://www.heritage.org/gender/
      commentary/sex-reassignment-doesnt-work-here-the-evidence.

94   Lisa Littman, "Parent Reports of Adolescents and Young Adults Perceived to
      Show Signs of a Rapid Onset of Gender Dysphoria," PLOS ONE, August 16,
      2018 . Retrieved February 12, 2021, from https://journals.plos.org/plosone/
      article?id=10.1371/journal.pone.0202330.

95   "Detransition Q&A (#1)," Pique Resilience Project, February 5, 2019, video, 27:32, https://www.piqueresproject.com/newsfeed/detransition-qa-1.

96   "The APS Modus Operandi: Ask Us No Questions, We'll Tell You No Lies," Arlington Parent Coalition, February 7, 2020, https://arlingtonparentcoa.wixsite.com/arlingtonparentcoa/post/the-aps-modus-operandi-ask-us-no-questions-we-ll-tell-you-no-lies.

97   Aaron Paquette, "Why Peer-to-Peer Selling Is Taking Off and What Companies Can Learn from It," MediaPost, July 10, 2014, https://www.mediapost.com/publications/article/229737/why-peer-to-peer-selling-is-taking-off-and-what-co.html.

98   Vicki Strange, Simon Forrest, and Ann Oakley, "Peer-Led Sex Education-Characteristics of Peer Educators and Their Perceptions of the Impact on Them of Participation in a Peer Education Programme," *Health Education Research* 17, no. 3 (June 2002): 327–337, https://academic.oup.com/her/article/17/3/327/658579.

99   Emery, L. R. (2016, December 15). *Sex ed taught by peers is effective, study says, so it's time to embrace it.* Bustle. https://www.bustle.com/articles/200097-sex-ed-taught-by-peers-is-effective-study-says-so-its-time-to-embrace-it.

100 "What Is Sex Education, Planned Parenthood, accessed June 24, 2024, https://www.plannedparenthood.org/learn/for-educators/what-is-sex-education; "Creating Safe and Welcoming Schools," Human Rights Campaign, accessed June 24, 2024, https://www.welcomingschools.org/.

101 Quoted in Doug Mainwaring, "Most Teachers Quite Disturbed about Their Unions' Push for Sexualization and Indoctrination of School Children," LifeSiteNews, October 10, 2019, https://www.lifesitenews.com/news/most-teachers-quite-disturbed-about-their-unions-push-for-sexualization-and-indoctrination-of-school-children.

102 "The State of the School 2020: Full Vigilance Required," Arlington Parent Coalition, March 2, 2020, https://arlingtonparentcoa.wixsite.com/arlingtonparentcoa/post/the-state-of-the-school-2020-full-vigilance-required; Cathy Ruse, C., *Sex Education in Public Schools: Sexualization of Children and LGBT Indoctrination* (Washington, DC: Family Research Council, 2020), https://downloads.frc.org/EF/EF20E22.pdf.

103 Geoff Herbert, "Sex Sells: 92 Percent of Top 10 Billboard Songs Are about Sex, Study Finds," G. (October 4, 2011, Syracuse.com, https://www.syracuse.com/entertainment/2011/10/billboard_top_10_songs_about_sex_suny_albany_study.html.

104 Rae Witte, "Sexism Sells: An Evolution of Selling Sex in Advertising," Nylon, February 5, 2020, https://www.nylon.com/sexism-in-advertising-2020.

105 "PG 13 Movie Rating," Parental Guide, accessed June 24, 2024, https://www.parentalguide.org/movie-ratings/pg-13/.

106 "Pornography," Enough Is Enough, accessed February 14, 2021, https://www.enough.org/stats_porn_industry.

107 Talking points: Increase in violence, National Center on Sexual Exploitation, August 16, 2016, https://endsexualexploitation.org/violence/.

108 D. Thompson, "Study Sees Link between Porn and Sexual Dysfunction," Web MD, May 12, 2017 (accessed February 14, 2021; no longer available), https://www.webmd.com/sex/news/20170512/study-sees-link-between-porn-and-sexual-dysfunction.

109 Louise Perry, "What Is Autogynephilia? An Interview with Dr. Ray Blanchard," Quillette, November 6, 2019, https://quillette.com/2019/11/06/what-is-autogynephilia-an-interview-with-dr-ray-blanchard/; *Diagnostic and Statistical Manual of Mental Disorders*, 5th ed. (Arlington, VA: American Psychiatric Association, 2013), 685, 818.

110 Miranda Yardley, "Pornography and Autogynephilia in the Narratives of Adult Transgender Males," May 15, 2017, Miranda Yardley website, https://mirandayardley.com/en/pornography-and-autogynephilia-in-the-narratives-of-adult-transgender-males/.

111 Jean C. Lloyd, "Why a Generation of Girls Is Fleeing Womanhood," Public Discourse, August 10, 2020, from https://www.thepublicdiscourse.com/2020/08/69452/.

112 Debra W. Soh, "Science Shows Sex Is Binary, Not a Spectrum," Real Clear Politics, October 31. 2018, https://www.realclearpolitics.com/articles/2018/10/31/science_shows_sex_is_binary_not_a_spectrum_138506.html#!.

113 Colin Wright, "JK Rowling Is Right — Sex Is Real and It Is Not a 'Spectrum,'" June 7, 2020, https://quillette.com/2020/06/07/jk-rowling-is-right-sex-is-real-and-it-is-not-a-spectrum/.

114 Ryan T. Anderson, "Sex Change: Physically Impossible, Psychosocially Unhelpful, and Philosophically Misguided," Public Discourse, March 5, 2018, https://www.thepublicdiscourse.com/2018/03/21151/.

115 Born in the Wrong Body? Transgender Trend, October 26, 2017, https://www.transgendertrend.com/born-in-the-wrong-body/.

116 Lillian Kwon, "Transgender Kid: God Made a Mistake," The Christian Post, April 27, 2007, https://www.christianpost.com/news/transgender-kid-god-made-a-mistake.html.

117 Margaret Thaler Singer, *Cults in Our Midst: The Hidden Menace of Our Everyday Lives* (San Francisco: Jossey-Bass, 1995), as excerpted at Cult Education Institute, accessed June 29, 2024, https://culteducation.com/group/1273-recovery/17912-cults-in-our-midst-leaving-a-cult-and-recoverings.html.

118 Rosanne Henry, "Dr. Robert J. Lifton's Eight Criteria for Thought Reform," Rosanne Henry, L.P.C., website, April 13, 2004, http://cultrecover.com/sites/default/files/pdfs/lifton8criteria.pdf.

119 Diane Ehrensaft, "How to Tell If Babies Are Transgender," Peachyo-
ghurt Genderfree, July 23, 2018, YouTube video, 3:11, https://youtu.be/
M7KBZeRC1RI.

120 Matt Hadro, "Scholar Ryan Anderson's Critique of Transgender Movement
Reportedly De-listed by Amazon," *National Catholic Register*, February 22,
2021, https://www.ncregister.com/cna/scholar-ryan-andersons-critique-of-
transgender-movement-reportedly-de-listed-by-amazon.

121 Henry, "Dr. Robert J. Lifton's Eight Criteria for Thought Reform."

122 Meghan Murphy, "Trans Activism Is Excusing and Advocating Violence
Against Women, and It's Time to Speak Up," Feminist Current, May 1, 2018,
https://www.feministcurrent.com/2018/05/01/trans-activism-become-
centered-justifying-violence-women-time-allies-speak/.

123 "San Francisco Public Library Hosts Transgender 'Art Exhibit' Featur-
ing Weapons Intended to Kill Feminists," Deep Green Resistance News
Service, May 1, 2018, https://dgrnewsservice.org/civilization/patriarchy/
male-violence/library-hosts-transgender-art-weapons-kill-feminists/.

124 "Model Policies for the Treatment of Transgender Students in Virginia's
Public Schools," Arlington Parent Coalition, January 9, 2021, https://arling-
tonparentcoa.wixsite.com/arlingtonparentcoa/post/model-policies-for-the-
treatment-of-transgender-students-in-virginia-s-public-schools.

125 Ryan T. Anderson, "Parents Denied Custody of Child for Refusing Support of
Transgenderism: Here's What You Need to Know," LifeSite News, February
20, 2018, February 20, https://www.lifesitenews.com/opinion/getting-a-
sense-of-the-brave-new-transgender-world-how-parents-can-have-the.

126 For descriptions of these two statutes, see "Family Educational Rights and
Privacy Act (FERPA)," U.S. Department of Education, last modified August
25, 2021, https://www2.ed.gov/policy/gen/guid/fpco/ferpa/index.html;
and "Regulations and Laws," Harvard University Office for Gender Equity,
accessed July 1, 2024, https://oge.harvard.edu/regulations-laws.

127 Maria Keffler, "The Six Steps a Predator Takes in Grooming a Child," Living on the Hill, February 5, 2021, https://uncommongroundmedia.com/
the-six-steps-a-predator-takes-in-grooming-a-child/.

128 "L'Oreal Sacks First Transgender Model Munroe Bergdorf," BBC, September
1, 2017, https://www.bbc.com/news/newsbeat-41127404; Quoted in A.
Aharon, "The Secret Tactics of Glitter Moms: A Tale of Betrayal and Grooming," Transgender Abuse, January 29, 2021, January 29 (accessed February
16, 2021; no longer available), https://www.transgenderabuse.org/post/
the-secret-tactics-of-glitter-moms-a-tale-of-betrayal-and-grooming.

129 Grace Chen, "Parental Involvement Is Key to Student Success," Public School
Review, updated Mary 20 2022, https://www.publicschoolreview.com/blog/
parental-involvement-is-key-to-student-success; Maggie Gallagher, "Why

Marriage Is Good for You," *City Journal* (Autumn 2000), https://www.city-journal.org/html/why-marriage-good-you-12002.html.

130 Graham Linehan, "Another Central Outlier: Rachel McKinnon," The Glinner Update, January 23, 2021, https://grahamlinehan.substack.com/p/another-central-outlier-rachel-mckinnon.

131 "Grooming," National Society for the Prevention of Cruelty to Children, accessed August 19, 2020, https://www.nspcc.org.uk/what-is-child-abuse/types-of-abuse/grooming/.

132 Malcolm Gladwell, "In Plain View," *New Yorker*, September 17, 2012, https://www.newyorker.com/magazine/2012/09/24/in-plain-view.

133 *Model School District Policy on Transgender and Gender Nonconforming Students* (Washington, DC: National Center for Transgender Equality and GLSEN, revised September 2018), 4, https://www.glsen.org/sites/default/files/2019-10/GLSEN-Model-School-District-Policy-Transgender-Gender-Nonconforming-Students.pdf.

134 Heather Brunskell-Evans, "The Billion Dollar Transgender Industry Masquerading as a Civil Rights Movement," Lipstick Alley, November 19, 2020, https://www.lipstickalley.com/threads/the-billion-dollar-transgender-industry-masquerading-as-a-civil-rights-movement.4117363/.

135 Colin Wright, "I'm Frequently Asked Why I Focus So Much on the Nature of Biological Sex," X (Twitter), March 4, 2020, https://twitter.com/swipewright/status/1235302606819467265.

136 "The School Counselor and Transgender/Gender-Nonconforming Youth," American School Counselor Association, 2016. This statement was updated in 2022: https://www.schoolcounselor.org/Standards-Positions/Position-Statements/ASCA-Position-Statements/The-School-Counselor-and-Transgender-Gender-noncon.

137 Debra Fulghum Bruce, "Grief and Depression," WebMD, August 28, 2022, https://www.webmd.com/depression/guide/depression-grief#1.

138 Fraser Myers, "My Battle with the Transgender Thoughtpolice: James Caspian on the Suppression of His Research into People Who Detransition," Spiked, February 22, 2019, https://www.spiked-online.com/2019/02/22/my-battle-with-the-transgender-thoughtpolice/.

139 Glenn Collins, "The Psychology of the Cult Experience," *New York Times*, March 15, 1982, https://www.nytimes.com/1982/03/15/style/the-psychology-of-the-cult-experience.html.

140 Liv Bridge, Detransitioners Are Living Proof the Practices Surrounding 'Trans Kids' Need Be Questioned," Feminist Current, January 9, 2020, https://www.feministcurrent.com/2020/01/09/detransitioners-are-living-proof-the-practices-surrounding-trans-kids-need-be-questioned/.

141 See 9:20–10:03 in "Detransition Q&A (#1)."

142 Rebecca Joy Stanborough, "What Types of Therapy Can Help Treat a Phobia?" Healthline, December 15, 2020, https://www.healthline.com/health/therapy-for-phobias.

143 JK Rowling, "Others Scorched for Lamenting Rising 'Intolerance,'" Al Jazeera, July 8, 2020, https://www.aljazeera.com/news/2020/7/8/j-k-rowling-others-scorched-for-lamenting-rising-intolerance.

144 Wilfred Reilly, "Are We in the Midst of a Transgender Murder Epidemic?" Quillette, December 7, 2019, https://quillette.com/2019/12/07/are-we-in-the-midst-of-a-transgender-murder-epidemic/.

145 Kendra Cherry, "Locus of Control and Your Life," Verywell Mind, updated June 24, 2024, https://www.verywellmind.com/what-is-locus-of-control-2795434.

146 Joseph Backholm, "Is Critical Theory Practical?" Breakpoint, May 5, 2020, https://breakpoint.org/is-critical-theory-practical/; Elizabeth Chuck, "University of Chicago: We Don't Condone Safe Spaces or 'Trigger Warnings,'" NBC News, August 25, 2016, https://www.nbcnews.com/news/education/university-chicago-we-don-t-condone-safe-spaces-or-trigger-n637721.

147 "Transgender Resources," GLAAD, accessed July 1, 2024, https://www.glaad.org/transgender/resources.

148 Erin Brewer, "Insights from a Detransitioner," March 25, 2021, YouTube video, 58:27, https://youtu.be/1FaYBRpe9Ok.

149 Information regarding this survey can be found at the bottom of the following web page: "Desist, Detrans & Detox," Partners for Ethical Care, accessed July 1, 2024, https://www.partnersforethicalcare.com/desist-detrans-detox.

150 Donald S. Yamagami, "Prosecuting Cyber-Pedophiles: How Can Intent Be Shown in a Virtual World in Light of the Fantasy Defense?" *Santa Clara Law Review*, 41, no. 2 (2000): 547–549, https://digitalcommons.law.scu.edu/cgi/viewcontent.cgi?article=1346&context=lawreview.

151 "About Us," Center for Child Protection, accessed July 1, 2024, https://centerforchildprotection.org/preventing-child-sexual-abuse/.

152 Banu Kucukemre Aydin, et al., "Frequency of Ambiguous Genitalia in 14,777 Newborns in Turkey," *Journal of the Endocrine Society* 3, no. 6 (April 24, 2019): pp. 1185–1195, https://pubmed.ncbi.nlm.nih.gov/31139765/.

153 "Changed Stories," Changed Movement, accessed July 1, 2024, https://changedmovement.com/stories.

Sophia Institute

Sophia Institute is a nonprofit institution that seeks to nurture the spiritual, moral, and cultural life of souls and to spread the gospel of Christ in conformity with the authentic teachings of the Roman Catholic Church.

Sophia Institute Press fulfills this mission by offering translations, reprints, and new publications that afford readers a rich source of the enduring wisdom of mankind.

Sophia Institute also operates the popular online resource CatholicExchange.com. *Catholic Exchange* provides world news from a Catholic perspective as well as daily devotionals and articles that will help readers to grow in holiness and live a life consistent with the teachings of the Church.

In 2013, Sophia Institute launched Sophia Institute for Teachers to renew and rebuild Catholic culture through service to Catholic education. With the goal of nurturing the spiritual, moral, and cultural life of souls, and an abiding respect for the role and work of teachers, we strive to provide materials and programs that are at once enlightening to the mind and ennobling to the heart; faithful and complete, as well as useful and practical.

Sophia Institute gratefully recognizes the Solidarity Association for preserving and encouraging the growth of our apostolate over the course of many years. Without their generous and timely support, this book would not be in your hands.

www.SophiaInstitute.com
www.CatholicExchange.com
www.SophiaTeachers.org

Sophia Institute Press is a registered trademark of Sophia Institute.
Sophia Institute is a tax-exempt institution as defined by the
Internal Revenue Code, Section 501(c)(3). Tax ID 22-2548708.